SHADES OF ENGAGEMENT

Shades *of* Engagement

~

Georgia O'Keeffe
and the
Erotic Landscapes
of Maui

DENNIS ALAN WINTERS

OUTPOST PRESS
PIONEER VALLEY, MASS.

OUTPOST
PRESS
AN IMPRINT OF WAYFARER BOOKS

Published in 2024 by Outpost Press, an imprint of Wayfarer Books
Cover Design and Interior Design by Wayfarer Books
Cover image © Dennis Alan Winters
Interior Images
Naoki Kutsunai, *Tao Valley*, Photograph, 1937.
Naoki Kutsunai, *The Canyon*, Photograph, 1937.
O'Keeffe Paints Reprinted with Permission.
For information on the Georgia O'Keeffe paintings reproduced in this publication
please see the backmatter for proper citation of each work.

TRADE PAPERBACK 978-1-965320-35-8
10 9 8 7 6 5 4 3 2 1

Look for our titles in paperback, ebook, and audiobook wherever books are sold.
Wholesale offerings for retailers available through Ingram.

PO Box 1601, Northampton, MA 01060

wayfarer@homeboundpublications.com

OUTPOST PRESS

For my family

Contents

When you read erotic symbols into my painting
you're really thinking about your own affairs.

—Georgia O'Keeffe

Georgia O'Keeffe   though you may not have painted erotic body parts
indeed   you were held captive by the erotic engagement of landscape itself.

—Dennis Alan Winters

I

Open Sea

1

Five Days

Yet,—wouldst thou the mountain find
Where this deity (Freedom) is shrined,
Who gives to seas and sunset skies
Their unspent beauty of surprise[1]

Georgia O'Keeffe—
passenger 27   age 51
sails first class from Los Angeles to Honolulu on Matson Company's
seafaring château   the SS *Lurline.*   Her fine   articulated fingers
curled around the coarse dark wood railing   she rolls with the Pacific.
The Hawaiian Pineapple Company   the *pre* of Dole Pineapple
is to cover all expenses.   In exchange   she'll paint pineapples
for their national pineapple promotion campaign:

> *Hospitable Hawai'i cannot send you*
> *its abundance of flowers or its sunshine.*
> *But it will send you something reminiscent of both—*
>
> *golden, fragrant Dole Pineapple Juice.*[2]

Humid subtropical Hawai'i had not been on her agenda.[3]
Having discovered New Mexico 23 years ago
having moved there a dozen years later
she began calling the high   wild   desert landscape   home.[4]

3

Her Ghost Ranch
the red & yellow cliffs
white buttes   silt-covered arroyos   Cerro Pedernal.   Even the dust
the storms   the desolation.   It was
where she felt reborn

where she felt most alive
where she'd know landscape as her own body
                   her body as landscape—
ridges like her spine
meanders like her hips
scarps like her brow.   Embodied as desert landscape.

Georgia O'Keeffe is not keen to see herself as water
nor to see herself as volcanic   for that matter
even if her passionate reverence for landscape is akin
to an explosive kind of volcanism.

On the other hand
painting Hawaiian pineapples
would be welcome respite from the continuing saga of obscene chatter
lurid innuendos   &   indiscreet critiques of her oils
exhibited by Stieglitz at 291   his New York City
art gallery
18 years ago   &   critics & friends alike
have not stopped regarding her oils as mere testaments
to Freud's carnal pronouncements:

Sexually explicit ...
Revelations of the most intimate ...
The world of woman turned inside out ...[5]

Exasperated   she'd countered:

> *My paintings erotic?   No way!*
> *That's something you yourself put into them.*
> *When you read erotic symbols into my paintings*
> *you're really talking about your own affairs!*[6]

> *Surely you jest*   they'd countered.

Squinting at the full moon's skip through pixilating waves
wind brushes her cheeks
wind braids her long   shiny black hair
wind whispers unfamiliar stanzas
signs its name on her pursed mouth

> *Aloha   our breath   together.*

Her pursed lips soften.

Freedom   bestowed by dawn.
Freedom   as broad as the sea.
Freedom   as vast as Space.
Freedom   she's not felt for an eternity

having agreed to paint Hawaiian pineapples
as long as she has the time
to paint what she wishes.

The Great Pineapple Escape of February 1939.

Five days at sea.

You'd find no tales of her voyage on the *Lurline*.
Apparently   the sea presents nothing of note for
Georgia O'Keeffe enthusiasts.   Biographers & critics
seemingly dismiss her journey
unless she paints.
Rather than considered an integral segment of her life
it's barely mentioned.
Not biographically significant   travel is assigned a minor role—
        a transition between affairs
        no relevance to creativity
        nor to artistic interpretation.

        Just as Thomas Malory dismissed Arthur's channel sailings
        between Brittany & the British Isles—neither battle
        debauchery   nor   pilgrims   crossing Arthur's path—
        when he wrote *Le Morte d'Arthur*.[7]

Five days at sea.

Not a molecular segment of time for those
whose fruits of livelihood derive from the sea
trained to synchronize with the operations of nature
knowing that nothing of the sea is simple
where survival depends upon anticipation
knowing injury & death is possible with each oncoming current
   or wave
where loss of life & vessel is delivered
   for disregard dismissal miscalculation or assumption
for those on the sea who
   cook clean cruise dig
   fish pump sail ship
   tug motor photo roughneck
   research survey & engineer
take nothing for granted.

Five days at sea.

No less than an eternity
for those forcibly severed from their homes
kidnapped & removed from their lands from their customs
from the people whom they loved & cherished
were loved & cherished in return.
Grounded by places once their own now distant memory.[8]

Although Georgia O'Keeffe is grounded by mesa & arroyo
of the continent not by canyons of the sea
five days at sea

will transform fruits of her labor
five days of perpetually moving landscape of winds & waves
        will purge internal contaminants
five days of sea's vast expanse
        will dissolve niggling emotional distress.
&   like the singular evocative line she delineates
in the center of her paintings—
        the line possessed with an uncanny knack to expose
        the expressive libido of her viewers
five days of Ocean Disc   &   Canopy of Sky
        will pry her own nether regions.

Five days of expanse
five days of freedom
five days of feeling truly alive
sanctifies her reservoir of inner silence
transforms her ways of being with landscape
her shades of engagement with landscape
her painting landscape with description   deepened by allegory
        allegory   deepened by evocative emotion
        emotion   deepened by invocation
        invocation   deepened by mystery—
The mystery of her becoming landscape.

Five days at sea.

Now   she only looks   &   paints nothing.
Even though a prolific letter writer   she pens a trifle

just brief notes to Stieglitz
packaged into one compact letter
posted when she arrives in Honolulu:

> *Sunday—There isn't any news—*
> *The Sea is big and blue—a few clouds—*
> *at night a beautiful moon.*
> *I haven't had much conversation with anyone—*
> *very satisfied to sit and   walk by myself—*
> *The air or boat motion—*
> *something makes me sleepy—It is much warmer*
> *today   I still wear my coat and woolen dress*
> *but many have turned out in quite summery things*[9]

Here—
I willingly disclose
this is not to be a bioscript of convenience.
Actual accounts of her intimate engagement
with Ocean Disc   &   Canopy of Sky
with the erotic landscapes of Maui
limited to memories captured by Patricia Jennings
        her 12-year-old guide
recorded in *Georgia O'Keeffe's Hawai'i*
limited to New York Botanical Garden's
Georgia O'Keeffe: Visions of Hawai'i
limited to her letters to Stieglitz preserved

in the Beinecke Rare Book and Manuscript Library
of Yale University
limited to *Georgia O'Keeffe: Catalogue Raisonné.*

       Limited to recordings of   earth   waters   &   sky.

Through this writing   drawn from biographical   &
autobiographical references
through this writing of her voyage   &
engagement with the Maui landscapes—
       its volcanic mountains   its valley   its waterfalls
my presumptuous attempt to touch her experience as mine
is suspended on a belief that in doing so
I might transform my own relationship with landscape.

If it's expanse she feels   can I feel the expanse?
If it's freedom she feels   can I feel the freedom?
then   what kind of freedom?
The freedom that arises from contemplating the vastness of sea & sky
       to be held by it
       to exalt in its inexpressible   incomparable   expanse
perhaps
freedom from the litany of salacious phenomena   &
other mental fabrications—
       ignorance   hatred & anger   stinginess
       hunger & gluttony   craving & jealousy

impeding an indivisible relationship with landscape
an unabashed continuity with the magnitude of this vast
360-degree   semisphere.

Freedom to transform whatever separates Georgia O'Keeffe   &   me
from our shades of engagement
with this Ocean Disc   &   Canopy of Sky

Would Georgia O'Keeffe's voyage be mine
as I write of hers?

2

Ocean Disc

The sea is so big it swallows geometry[10]

SS *Lurline* departs the protected harbor.
Calm waters.   Soothing departure.   Somnolent sleep.
Not so the following morning.
The open sea startles passengers not accustomed to
proclamations of the Pacific.
Bolted by the turbulence   their inside   like outside   roughshod.
Vomiting her first breakfast
Georgia O'Keeffe attempts a second.
It's difficult keeping food down.
However raucous the winds & waters
they can't confine her to her cabin.
Unlike others   she makes her way out
remains on deck most of the day.
By midafternoon   the ocean is calm.

Monday—It has been much warmer today—
I sat in the sun and I sat in the shade and I walked—
That is all—
Talked to a few people—Nothing interesting—
It is really a way to rest if you want to rest—
I am liking it—

And wondering about you as I got to bed early—
It is windy and drafty since it is dark—"

Georgia O'Keeffe has no interest in the ship's luxurious stylish interior
her first-class lanai suite notwithstanding.
The three upper decks of art deco décor
opulent showrooms of refined Hawaiian elegance
carved cherrywood panels & glass-tiled saloons
lacquer murals   glass-beaded curtains   sleek lighting
chic passengers doling out salon pleasures
          like glossy fashion idols
fur capes wrapped loosely over tailored suits
jazz bands   dancers   singers
staterooms of luxurious comfort
white inlaid dressers   woven wool carpets   wicker chairs & decks—
          distractions.

Reluctantly   she'd accept Captain C. A. Berndtson's invitation
to join him at the captain's table
in the opulent Waikiki Dining Room
for a many-course dinner
served on porcelain dishware rimmed with sterling silver—
          fantasies of no import.

She reclines in the sun on the wood slatted deck chairs
walks the moonlit upper deck.   Watches the silence.
When conversation tempts   she averts her gaze   &   walks away.
She'd miss engaging with Amelia Earhart

her Lockheed Vega airplane secured on deck   by five years.
She'd miss Elvis by 18.

Northeast trade winds rustle the water.

She takes measure of the sea on which she sails.
Neither clouds   coast   nor   mountains impede her view.
Nothing but   ocean   as far as she can see.
A circular disc whose perimeter is three & six-tenths nautical miles
away.
From the upper deck   perched higher   the perimeter of the disc
appears one & four-tenths nautical miles farther.

Assigning distance to the perimeter assumes it's reachable.
Regardless of the intent with which the SS *Lurline* steams
on its westerly course   toward this perimeter
the closer *Lurline* seems
the farther the perimeter recedes.
Mathematicians call this perception of movement in space
asymptote   approaching   &   never reaching.

Perhaps the horizon advances
while *Lurline*   like a mirage   recedes.

Uncertain that the sea extends beyond the perimeter
        sky   its spherical canopy.   From here
can she measure a boundary   a line   between ocean's end
&   beginning   of   sky?

On a two-dimensional ocean plane
a measurable distance from a measurable point helps make sense
of immensity
a degree of assurance there's a   *where*   in which to be present.
Without a reference   without knowing where she's placed
how difficult it must be to meditate a
"right here"   "right now."

The infinite makes no sense at all.

This undefined   indefinable place
other than swells   its pulse of motion
the sea offers no defining characteristics   no sense of bearing.

There's nothing to grasp
no piece of land to identify as her own
no canyon in which to be absorbed.
There's no wash   no cliff   no mesa   no canyon   no arroyo
no granite   no lava   no basalt   no sandstone   no uranium
no sage   no cacti   no mesquite   no piñon   no juniper
There's no buffalo grass   no bunch grass   no needle grass
no tumbleweed
          no Jimson   no cottonwood   &   no aspen.
There are no iron oxides   &   no oxidized ochres.
no Chaco Canyon   &   no Canyon de Chelly.

In the same way
there's no strip of white beach washed by rolling waves

no molten rock pounded by breaking surf
no undulating hills incised by dark green valleys
neither mist-covered canyon nor mist-covered mountain.
There's not even a radiant   spiritually endowed   cosmologically
centric
       smoking volcanic peak.
There's not one body of land that she can name.

Likewise
there's no mark   no scarecrow   nor   topographic relief
pointing this way or that
nothing of earth's solid tangibility with which to grasp.
With nothing to grasp   how can somewhere be known as
       someplace?
With no place defined   pointing neither this way nor that
how can she know where she is?
With no   *where* to be   are there   &   has she
       boundaries?

Unobstructed   unafraid
she doesn't reach for anything   out there
or   anywhere   &   so concludes
this must be freedom that she's found
       &
inhabiting that freedom
notwithstanding the swells harboring memories of her
Space-tended seductions
she recalls no landscape comparable to this.

Not the big desert outside Canyon   Texas
she'd actually likened to the ocean.
Not the sandy stretch of beach along York Beach   Maine
marking the edge of earth.[12]
Not New Mexico's naked boldness.
No other landscape has prepared her for this vast expanse of Space
          the mere lack of obstruction.

With nothing about it that she must grasp   she's not lost.
Extending her eyes outward to sea   &   upward to Space
she senses it as a vessel of vast unknowable opportunities
&   possibilities
          now released.

Just as ancient & contemporary fundamentalists vision the world
as a flat disc   center of all existence
Georgia O'Keeffe beholds the Ocean Disc as a chronicle of narratives.

Narrative number one:
Georgia O'Keeffe sails upon Homer's shield of Achilles.
Like Achilles   the sea projects invincibility
however   when the arrow of wisdom strikes Achilles' heel
his belief in immortality   his deluded foundation   collapses.

Narratives two   to   seven:

Georgia O'Keeffe sails upon the flat Ocean Disc of early Egypt

the Ocean Disc of Mesopotamia

the Ocean Disc of Israelites

the Ocean Disc of Herodotus

the Ocean Disc of ancient Norse & Germanic

the Ocean Disc of Hecataeus of Miletus

   all surrounding the earth.

Narratives eight   &   nine:

Georgia O'Keeffe sails upon cosmological layers of

Hindu Puranas   &   Buddhist *Abhidharma-kosa.*

A disc   appearing at the beginning of time   14 billion years ago

owed to the mind & collective karma of all sentient beings

the natural operative process of cause & effect

appearing each & every moment. The period called Formation.

   Collective imprints of   I want   I don't want   I don't care.

A disc

owed to the mind & collective karma of all sentient beings.

   Collective imprints of   I want   I don't want   I don't care

subtle energy-winds of motion   &   subtle energy-winds of rest

intensify   &   produce a great wind disc supported by Space.

Vigorous storms burst upon the wind disc   forming a great water disc.

Cyclones strike the upper part of the water disc

coagulate as a great gold disc.

Dynamic tempests draw up protuberates of immense proportion.

      They erupt   &   convert into mountains.

      They attain marvelous heights.

From this   arises the golden disc

      Cakravāla.

In the center of *Cakravāla*

Mt. Sumeru   rises 80,000 *yoganas* into the sky

surrounded by nine circular golden mountain ranges.

Between the mountains   eight great oceans.

The eponymous iron mountain *Cakravāla* surrounds all.

The cosmological arrangement of four continents

nine circular golden mountain ranges   &   Mt. Sumeru   .

owed to the mind & collective karma of all sentient beings.[13]

      Collective imprints of   I want   I don't want   I don't care.

Cakravāla means   "wheel of mountains."

Cakravāla means   the entire universe.

Cakravāla means   Ocean Disc   &   Canopy of Sky.

      Collective imprints of   I want   I don't want   I don't care.

Were this Pacific one of the nine great oceans

between cosmological mountain ranges

to what depths could she penetrate?   What mysteries beyond?

Georgia O'Keeffe sees no iron mountain range of the *Cakravāla*

She sees no edge of golden disc.

She sees only surface.

Fortunately   the edge continues to recede
&   she'll not fall off.

Pacific Ocean marine forecast:
Northwest winds 10 to 20 knots   becoming southwest 10 knots in the
afternoon
wind waves 2 to 3 feet
west swells 4 to 6 feet at 13 seconds
strong Southern Oscillation Index of +1.20 indicating
a stronger La Niña.[14]

3
Okéanos

What is the parentage of the sea?
What does the sea parent?   Borrowing
a stream of the sea's consciousness   inspired by
a stream of Hesiod's eighth century BCE Greek *Theogony:*

If there were an "In the Beginning"
Beginning would cite the mystic fruit of non-inherence
                consciousness itself   so engaged
with the nurturing & nourishing progenitor of all species.
                The operations of nature (Gaia)
arising   abiding   dissolving
                Causal Links of Change
                Expressed as Desire (Eros).

Arising   fruits of non-inherence
spheres of pure Darkness (Erebos)   &   Black Night.
                Rest.
Darkness & Night unite
& Night births Ether & Day.
                Motion.

Gaia births her celestial wrap (Ouranos)
the limitless sphere of Space   the heavens

    &   the visible cerulean Sky
          witnessed & beyond witness   both.

Gaia births her interior—
her 2,200-mile thick core
& 1,800-mile-thick mantle of magma (Tartaros) & her exterior—
          her mountainous crust of continental & oceanic plates
          their continuous migration over crystalline-liquid layers
               of upper mantle.

Gaia also births the lifeless Hadean Sea (Pontos).

Hadean Sea transforms into the enriched Archean Sea
unites with Gaia   &   produces the seas—
          their bounties   wonders   dangers & whirlwinds.
Above   they produce the rainbows & glories
          of amber-tinged clouds.

Gaia releases gases from her magma.
gases unite with Ouranos   the Sky.   Their mating
produces Atmosphere   where waters condense & fall as rain.
Rain births Okéanos   composite of all majestic salty waters
          of the earth
          &   Tethys   fresh bodies of inland lakes   springs   aquifers
          &   the ground.

Gaia & Ouranos unite   &   Gaia births storms & hurricanes.

&   again   Gaia & Ouranos unite   &   Gaia births time (Kronos)

transforming instability into the regularity of ebb & flow

the syncopation of tempos   melodies   &   harmonics.

Now vast Okéanos surrounds the earth.

Now vast Okéanos is deemed hospitable for habitation.

Now vast Okéanos unites with Tethys

their consummation cause to nurture & nourish—

       all facets of life & death

       all offspring of flux & motion[15]

       all immortals & mortals—

       the 3,000 slender-ankled daughters

       who roam & hunt the earth

       &   depths of waters   alike: the many tumbling

       &   rushing rivers

       &   seas   &   springs   &   deep wells.

       All offspring of Okéanos & Tethys

       the extent & expanse of their numbers & habitats so difficult

       for mortals to recite their sum

       the total of their names.[16]

4

Waves Are the Practice of Water

*According to the stories of ancient mariners, the sea was once still,
an immense lake without waves or ripples, and it could only be navi-
gated by paddle. Then a canoe, lost in time, arrived from the other side
of the world and found the island where the breezes lived. The mariners
captured them and carried them off and obliged them to blow. The
canoe rode on the captive breezes, and the mariners, who had spent
centuries paddling and paddling, could at last lie down to sleep. They
never awakened. The canoe crashed against a rocky cliff. Ever since,
the breezes wander the globe in search of their lost island home. Trade
winds and monsoons and hurricanes roam the seven seas, in vain. To
avenge that long-ago kidnapping, they sometimes sink the ships that
cross their path.*[17]

Somewhere   beyond the visible
in the midst of the nighttime maritime play
Breeze excites the warm Pacific air
&   wakes Ocean's skin.
Ocean's skin stretches.
Ocean's skin yawns.
Ocean's skin rustles.
Breeze intensifies   &   becomes Wind.
Wind intensifies   &   becomes Storm.

Storm agitates waters below Ocean's skin

producing a mélange of waves above.

Some waves remain infantile.

Some waves grow herculean.

Storm churns Ocean in all manner in all directions.

Water molecules spin   shift   &   gyrate

against one another.   A convoluted aqueous staccato.

The whirling convoluted aqueous staccato of molecules produce foam.

Foam congeals into froth.

Froth gives birth

to Aphrodite.

Inspired by Hesiod's *Theogony:*

From their birth day   the offspring of Gaia-Earth & Ouranos-Sky

are cursed by a contentious relationship with their father.

Against the will of Gaia-Earth

Ouranos-Sky imprisons each child within her womb

severed from contact with light.

To foil the malevolence of Ouranos-Sky

Gaia-Earth   with her youngest son Kronos-Time

plan   &   carry out their scheme—

Kronos-Time hides in ambush with sickle in hand

awaits   with sickle in hand

for Ouranos-Sky to seek coitus with Gaia-Earth.

When Ouranos-Sky stretches upon Gaia-Earth

concealed Time   grabs Ouranos-Sky with his left hand

castrates the genitals of Ouranos-Sky with his right hand

&   throws the genitals into stormy Okéanos.

      The mixture—

      primal male ingredients of Ouranos-Sky

      primal female ingredients of Okéanos

produces a chemical reaction of unprecedented dimension—

Okéanos surges with marvelous churning & foaming.

From this churning & foaming   the birth of love & beauty

in psyches of people   &   landscape.

      This love & beauty   is   Aphrodite

&   like the boundless expanse of the sea

the Greeks give the name   Aphrodite

to boundless love & beauty.

Sometime later   the Romans will say

beauty & sexual rapture are created

from the froth-making of the sea.

for her name actually means

      "from the churning of *aphros*"   or   "sea foam."[18]

Storms knead Ocean.

Frothing & foaming waves reshape Ocean's appearance

its shape & personae   on and near the surface

Wave profiles shorten   more elliptical than round

in colonies of similar height   clustered together

waves swarm together like intimates

cavort together   tease together   as they

gradually parcel themselves   equal distance between.

Each wave now identifies as a swell.

Winds shove equally distant swells into clusters.
Clusters   called wave trains   converge onto impromptu tracks
one cluster following another
like coupled cars of railway stock.

Wind kisses Ocean's surface
Ocean   agitated by the affection
responds   &   transforms energy into cyclical orbs of waves & swells.
        While appearing as if waves   &   swells
        propel Ocean's surface   &   objects floating upon it
        they don't.
The sequence of waves   &   swells
is the pulse of energy propelled across Ocean's surface.
Water remains (relatively) still.
        The rotation of waves & swells is its natural practice.[19]

Somewhere between Los Angeles & Honolulu
on a long day's journey   toward distant shores
a train of swells schedules a rendezvous with Georgia O'Keeffe
sailing first-class on the seafaring château   SS *Lurline.*
Her fine   articulated fingers
curled around the coarse dark wood railing   she rolls with the Pacific.
Approaching the ship   a wave train harbors the potential
to upset her tranquil state of mind   if not her stomach.   However
Georgia O'Keeffe isn't easily undone by natural phenomena.

Carrying both customary   &   the otherwise unusual
ocean-borne fodder   putrid & life-bearing   both

a train of swells appears to harbor something curiously improbable.
Georgia O'Keeffe watches a swell advance.   Intently watches
a swell unfold a memory that surfs upon its skin
            a memory of seduction by immense Space.

As the seafaring château   SS *Lurline*   propels forward
Georgia O'Keeffe cruises through memory after memory.
A swell harboring one memory following a swell harboring another
they surf past the ship's bow   they scamper alongside.
Swell following swell   memory following memory.
She times their advance by the periodicity between crests—
            13 seconds.

Swell   following   swell
travels to an unknown coast where it will wash ashore
will erode & replenish a beach   or
cascade against rock   wear it down   &
release her memory to the land.
Perhaps a memory will wash ashore on a Maui beach
where she'll reengage with remnants of who she was.

Sometimes a swell carrying one memory's signature
folds into an ensuing swell harboring an ensuing memory
the first swallowing the curling & folding of the second.
Scents of each memory soaked with scents of the sea
enveloped by Aphrodite's froth.

Each swell mirrors a moment of her life.
No two mirrors are the same.
       Past becomes present.

An advancing swell harbors a memory of seduction of
glaciated hills & marshes   &
the Sun Prairie   Wisconsin   dairy farm   her birth home
its bands of funny cigar-shaped drumlins made of
extruded glacial deposits   cattail marshes between
the sudden darkening summer storm
abbreviating an expansive undulating horizon.

A second advancing swell   harbors a memory of seduction of
secret   intimate spaces   penetrating her jack-in-the-pulpit
       as if she's looking at a flower for the very first time.
She carefully places the tip of her pencil on the tip of the spathe
the flower's hood   enclosing the flower.
Wonders how to compose her next move   then
tenderly delineates the purple stripes up and over the hood
       pauses   momentarily   &
slides down the curving nape of the pulpit   the flower's back.
Wrapping her pencil around one edge
       pauses—
then slips in & through the fine textured lining of cilia
plunging deeply into the spathe
toward the proud spadix   the flower's stalk wrapped within.
The tiny flower's anatomy urges the male zone upward

toward the top   the female zone toward the bottom
a sterile zone between them.

   Jack becomes her teenage beloved.

Georgia O'Keeffe is dismayed
sorely remembers it's none other than her high school art teacher who
manipulates her looking at jack-in-the-pulpit in that seditious way.
She doesn't like the look of that teacher at all
   that skinny   bright-eyed spinster
   probably not much older than Georgia O'Keeffe herself—
her pulled-back hair covered by that silly hat of hers
with its artificial violets &   yet
it's the first time Georgia O'Keeffe is taught to examine details
the first time she looks at a flower
with the thought of drawing or painting it &
she doesn't like that this teacher is the source
of her newly discovered attention to detail—
   no   she doesn't like that teacher at all.[20]

Even so
this is Georgia O'Keeffe's introduction to the delineation of
outline   composition & color   speaks to her sensuality
speaks to who she is
cultivates the visual choreographic score of her persona—
   inviting contacting longing desiring coveting exploring
   enveloped by the subtle mysteries of Space.

A third advancing swell   harbors a memory of seduction of
the silence of the vast Texas Panhandle
the utter flatness of the plains   the extraordinary immensity.
More like Ocean than Ocean itself.
The raw desert sand & gravel underfoot   deposited by
340-million-year-old Devonian seas
consolidated as bedrock   eventually broken down
then carried by a mighty river flushed by monsoon-drenched
mountains
of Pangaea 225 million years ago.
Hot days cool nights   limitless land.
Except for thousand-foot-deep slits of the Palo Duro Canyon
deep vertical slices through the horizontal expanse
there's nothing else in sight— no houses   no hills   no trees
nothing marring the horizon circling far away where earth meets Space
a perimeter of no-beginning-no-end.   No matter
Arthur Wesley Dow has helped free her from three-dimension
painting.[21]

And the Texas night sky—the black canopy that vibrates like a jewel.
The deepest colors hovering directly above in the center of the sky.
Colors she could only imagine were she to find herself
in the deepest of Ocean's trenches   sunsets lighting the canopy
curving gray-blue clouds blazing
sheet lightning followed by zigzagging flashes across it.   Otherwise
endless chartless   signless   Space.

Nothing to reference

but stars   distance measured in light-years
however long it takes for its light to reach her—
        tens of light-years   hundreds of light-years.
Time has no meaning   so she looks   just looks
just prairie   &   sky.   Even so
she craves to touch Space   as if touching herself.[22]

Now a fourth advancing swell   harbors a memory of seduction of
the repetitive play of waves on the Maine coast shore at York Beach.
The oscillation of the sea   waves appearing from beyond edges
of the known world
treeless & mountainless Ocean
marking boundaries between heaven & earth.
A line marking beginnings of   time   &   Space.

The long steady roll of greenish-gray breakers.
    Spray like the manes of wild horses flying back
    from the top of each wave.
    Whitecaps rolling ever so seemingly slowly ambling their way
    towards the beach like oversized sea serpents and then
    suddenly
    flashing onto the shore as turbulent roaring breakers
    instantaneous raucous male energy inserting its presence
    then depleting just as quickly
    transformed into female loveliness
    as its foam gradually spreads across the sand
    subtly filling the curving contours of the beach
        so like her own spreading.   Waiting
        for the next powerful breaker that was male—[23]

A fifth advancing swell   harbors a memory of
her first voyage   most unpleasant   to recuperate in Bermuda
from emotionally charged marital entanglements with Stieglitz
She remembers nothing   of the Bermuda sea   of the cruise   of the sky.
Sick in her bed sick in her cabin for entire days eats & drinks nothing.
Of the island   nothing makes sense.   The ground sounds hollow
when she walks on the pitted limestone bedrock
its blanket of airy coral like an unsupported platform
she maneuvers carefully lest she fall off the earth.[24]

Georgia O'Keeffe's intimacy
with the coast of Maine
with the Wisconsin prairies
with the New Mexico desert
with the Texas Panhandle plains
doesn't follow the same rhythm of the warm Pacific Sea—
        its excited breezes   its awakening Ocean surface
        its winds   storms   waves & swells harboring memories.
Even so   do those memories of intimacy & immensity really matter?
        She says that where she was born   where & how she lives
        is unimportant.   It's what she does with where she is
        that matters.[25]

Female swells & male waves   churn the private parts of the Pacific.
The whistle of the male dolphin & chirp of the female.

5

Horizon

To find the feeling of infinity on the horizon line[26]

As a student at Teacher's College Columbia University
Georgia O'Keeffe hears Arthur Wesley Dow say:

> *Georgia O'Keeffe   begin with a line.*[27]

Now   five days at sea   Arthur Wesley Dow's line
    is the horizon.
This line   this horizon   defines the boundary
between Ocean Disc   &   Canopy of Sky
    This line   this horizon   has no thickness at all

    The word   horizon   is derived from the Greek *kyklos.*
    Kyklos means   "bounding circle."
        &
    The word   horizon   is derived from the verb *horizō.*
    Horizō means   "to divide"   &   "to separate."
        &
    The word   horizon   is derived from the noun *oros.*
    Oros means   "boundary"   or   "landmark."

The word   horizon   means   as far as the eye can see.

Horizon is not a simple two-dimensional line.
Georgia O'Keeffe's line is not the same as horizon.
Neither is it two dimensions.
Her line is a beguiling invitation to unseen fantasies—

      a flirt   a seductive beckoning

      a slight turn of a corner   around a curve

      anticipation   revelation

      penetration

      consummation   wishes rewarded

      absorbed into landscape's private domain

      into the private parts of Georgia O'Keeffe.

Horizon is not a simple two-dimensional line.
Horizon is a zone of contentious unpredictable encounters

      between Ocean Disc   &   Canopy of Sky.

Georgia O'Keeffe   as does Gaston Bachelard
watches tightened tensions from the machinations
between Ocean Disc   &   Canopy of Sky
machinations to breach the horizon.[28]

      My side   your side.

Breaching the horizon
Ouranos-Sky imprisons its offspring
within Gaia's Archean interior   inhibits
the arising   abiding   &   dissolving
of ancient seas   its magnified swells   &   rivers

the matchless strength of storms   thunder   lightning
while trees   waters   &   mountains in their natural acts
penetrate Ouranos-Sky   make Sky invisible
        the malevolence is foiled.[29]

Breaching the horizon
Ouranos-Sky   &   Okéanos-Sea soak each other's domain
with their respective chemical constituents—
        Ouranos-Sky's consignment of CO_2
        Okéanos-Sea's consignment of O_2
the sea's phytoplankton   kelp   &   algal plankton providing
up to 80 percent of Gaia's O_2 to be inhaled by all living things.

Breaching the horizon
Ouranos-Sky   &   Okéanos-Sea soak each other's domain
with their respective Prismacolor spectacles—
Tuscans   vermilions   crimsons   slates   umbers (burnt and raw)
&   grays   (warm medium gray   cold light gray   Payne's gray).

Breaching the horizon
Ouranos-Sky penetrates Okéanos-Sea
clouds of cool precipitate
        as if Space were transformed into form   as
Okéanos-Sea envelops Ouranos-Sky
clouds of warm evaporate
        as if form were transformed into Space.
        The natural erotic engagement of complementary pairs.

Breaching the horizon

Ouranos-Sky animates with male motion & female rest   &

Okéanos-Sea animates with female rest & male motion

Ouranos-Sky motion & rest isn't possible

      without Okéanos-Sea rest & motion

Okéanos-Sea motion & rest isn't possible

      without Ouranos-Sky rest & motion.

      The natural erotic engagement of complementary pairs.

Breaching the horizon

like the engagement of Hindu's Garuda-Sky & Nāga-Sea—

Okéanos-Nāga-Sea agitates vigorously

when saturated by Ouranos-Garuda-Sky's storms & strikes

      Sea as male.

Ouranos-Garuda-Sky demurs demonically

when saturated by Okéanos-Nāga-Sea's subtle evaporates

      Sky as female.

Gender identities of Okéanos-Nāga-Sea & Ouranos-Garuda-Sky

are mobile   &   not exclusively binary.

      The natural erotic engagement of complementary pairs.

Horizon mediates transactions between Ocean Disc & Canopy of Sky

mediates tendencies abiding in their respective hemispheres—

vertical	with	horizontal
project	with	embrace
supply	with	receive
probe	with	reveal
precipitate	with	evaporate
wet	with	dry
form	with	Space

The natural erotic engagement of complementary pairs.

Horizon is the liminal landscape exemplar
amplifies spiritual transformation   &   renewal
where distinct formations meet   &   speak with each other—

       the intersection of geological chapters

       the bastion of topographic frontiers

       the hinterland of ecological systems.

The liminal landscape is transactional ground—
amplifies spiritual transformation   &   renewal
where Georgia O'Keeffe is most intimate with the operations of
nature—

       materials composing lands   waters   &   skies

       evolutionary   arising   abiding   &   dissolving

       time taken   is taking   will take   to construct & erode
its moments   &   changes—

       moments of celestial transformation

       conjunctions of planetary bodies

       solstice & equinox

       sunrise & sunset.

The liminal landscape is transactional ground—
amplifies spiritual transformation   &   renewal
to construct the metaphorical universe
to construct temples   &   shrines   &   gardens
to conduct ceremonies   &   personal quests
to conduct meditation retreats
to strengthen bonds between
   who we are   &   where we are.

Where Georgia O'Keeffe is most keenly aware of the totality of life
feels most   open   alive   free
feels most "Georgia O'Keeffe."

Horizon is the liminal landscape exemplar.

The liminal landscape is transactional ground—
amplifies spiritual transformation   &   renewal
where awareness of life forms of female nature   broadens
   (or tends to focus)
   by meeting life forms of male nature
where awareness of life forms of male nature   focuses
   (or tends to broaden)
   by meeting life forms of female nature

Where sensitivity to rising heightens   by encountering falling
where sensitivity to motion magnifies   by encountering repose
where sensitivity to solidity strengthens   by encountering fluidity.

Where dry meets wet   heat meets cold
Space meets form.

Where growth & life   meet decay & death.

Where the essence of subtle energies
ply the earth   in the waters   &   on the winds.

Where pilgrims make sacred pacts with Divinity
charging the atmosphere with the power of those pacts
absorbing the energy of the landscape   breathing it—
&   as it flows through their veins
strikes chords in their hearts   to make them sing.[30]

Horizon is the liminal landscape exemplar.

Were Georgia O'Keeffe to paint the liminal landscape of horizon
would she paint a beyond the edge of earth?
Would she paint liberation from two-dimensional geometric confines?
Would she paint the hidden past?   Constant present?
Spilling potential?

What happens to Georgia O'Keeffe   far   far away?
Five days at sea?

6

Cumulus Charade

Day-old almost-full waxing gibbous moon in the low   western sky
reflects morning light into sea's spray.
Venus   brightest celestial body in the sky   rises
with the eastern dawn   &   slips through the stem of Libra.
Mars   a pin of red within Virgo.
Mercury   closest to the sun   (though appears farthest away)
too dim for Georgia O'Keeffe's naked eye.[31]

White wispy clouds—

The world turns.
The sun slips from its nocturnal trip around the underside of the earth
that intense moment of the morning's new light
that liminal moment between   dawn   &   day
that simple pin of light   that orb of pure red sun.
Georgia O'Keeffe pinches the virginal simplicity between her
thumb & finger.

Morning colors mirror familiar pangs.   She muses:
Are temperaments of the sea akin to my terrestrial moodiness?
How to paint elation & depression under the Pacific Canopy of Sky?
Hints of deep reds?

Nighttime blues?
        Casts of gray-purples?
                Prisms of deep maroons?
Extremes she knows too well.

Discrete white clouds—
like schools of long thin scaled lancelets
minute bulbs rising from the top
sides like small wings   or fins
mouths folding into clouded hoods   no distinct heads
tails pointing to the rear   like lances
flat underneath
        phylum *Chordata*
        subphylum *Cephalochordata*
        class *Leptocardii*
        order *Amphioxiformes*
        family *Branchiostomidae*
        species *Branchiostoma*
hovering low   near Ocean's surface.

Discrete light chiffon clouds—
riding the northeast trade winds
hover behind the lancelets like schools of pipefish
specifically   velvet ghost pipefish   species *Solenostomus.*
Generally difficult to find except near the sponge corals they inhabit
they assume the demeanor of their host
their skin mimics textures & colors of their surrounding
whites   pinks   &   brilliant red sponges.

Georgia O'Keeffe grabs a stubby lateral fin.
Too small   she lets it fly.

Discrete pink & alabaster clouds—
like long ribbons of taffeta
&   other discrete white clouds   like 2,000-feet-long giant kelp
70 feet below the surface   processed to emulsify   &
stabilize   ice cream   syrup   salad dressing   &
medicinal supplements when iron or iodine is needed.
They want to kiss her face.

Discrete straight strings of lacy white clouds—
one splits from the others   a maverick among peers
an unaligned renegade   shaped like a three-quarter circle
like a Japanese *enso*.   It signifies—
        in dependence upon causes & conditions
        anything is possible.
An auger for Georgia O'Keeffe   were she to believe in apparitions.

Discrete cotton clouds—
envelopes of soft fleece   inner sanctuaries.
Circular strands of fur flowing ever so slowly
like a play of aerial teddy bears   &   velveteen rabbits
like a slow sultry sensual bolero
like the wisp of a ghost that seems to take
an embarrassingly long time to travel
over a minute distance   surveying its aerial domain
like the slow movement   &   rest of a t'ai chi master

whose awareness of body   speech   &

patience of mind disarms the winds around her.

However   Georgia O'Keeffe knows clouds aren't really like this.

These stratospheric-faring behemoths

travel   &   transform over great distance

taking mere moments of time   intense tempests raging within.

They'll severely damage aircraft   toss crew & passengers

to an undesired end.

        Pilots avoid them.

Discrete light gray corkscrew clouds   outlined—

like orange three-dimension comics

like bliss swirls rotating in the belly chakra of a Buddhist *tantrika.*

Orbs of white fleece surrounding patches of open blue sky

like mantles she'd wear around her neck

like the pelvis bones she'd paint   finding them

years later on the grounds of her New Mexico desert at Ghost Ranch.

        Pinks like her *Pelvis I 1944 & Pedernal 1945.*

Discrete puerile clouds—

yellows   ochres   oranges   reds   solid whisks of Payne's gray.

But no stubby puerile puffballs cloud the sky.

A subtropical palette.

Neither coast nor mountains puncture these discrete clouds

nor do they puncture the parade of syncopated cumulus clouds

a rhythmic cadence

their motation like layers of harmonic chords.   An aerial display
were it sound   like a scale played by jazz percussionists
clouds arising   abiding   &   dissolving
motifs keeping time to heavens' beating heart.

A visual bebop   a regular rhythmic pulse—

  CRASH DOOMPH SWASH

Not audible   not thunder.
The tempo—
 mounding drum rolls   marks of linear pinks & light blue-grays
 hints of deep maroons   roll to the pulse of waves below
 braiding swirls of water vapor   rising
 absorbed by the parading cloud mass   like loose ruffled quilts
 hi-hats ride eighth notes   mounding white domes expand at top
  bass drums on beats one & three
  snares on beats two & four
  domes of billowing clouds   thrusting deep gorges between
   the aerial cleavage.
She taps her finger to the visual cadence.

The cumulus parade refashions as a writhing white dragon
wings kicking swirls of vapor   the airborne Garuda.
Geological millennia ago   these aerial dragons
devised ingenious mechanical devices   insurance they'd birth
  &   rebirth   &   rebirth themselves
invigorating libidos to amplify mass—

the rhythmic cadence of their flapping wings
causing the surface of the sea to evaporate
vapor drawn up from Ocean
air condensing as elongated mounds
upon the dragon's crest & crown
folding into serrations   ridges of its back.
A symbiotic agreement to which Ocean & Sky still abide
clouds return the reservoir of water to the sea below
          as rain.

While Georgia O'Keeffe calls dragons of Sky   male
&   Ocean's churning & foaming   female
dragon's receiving is a female act   &   Ocean's giving is a male act
          feeding & nurturing the other.
          The natural erotic engagement of complementary pairs.

Like their terrestrial cousins   the writhing mountain ridges
the aerial dragons modulate the horizontality of the sky
their elevated profiles like tracks of a roller coaster.
Seeing this   what might Georgia O'Keeffe think of
Rainer Maria Rilke's take on dragons?

> Let us not forget the ancient myths at the outset of humanity's
> journey, the myths about dragons that at the last moment transform into
> princesses. Perhaps all the dragons of our lives are princesses who are only
> waiting to see us act just once with beauty and courage. Perhaps every ter-
> ror is, in its deepest essence, something that needs our recognition or help.[32]

The cumulus parade now refashions as a winged stallion
gallops through its aerial equestrian domain
its emboldened mane praised by high atmospheric winds.
That stallion would be Pegasus.
The name Pegasus   &   its natural way of being
emerges from Ocean's springs   evaporating seas
regenerating the dragon's beating wings.

Pegasus' paternal grandfather was the fertile flow of time.
Pegasus' father was Poseidon   the cyclical operation
of rising   &   falling seas   &   the irregular quaking of the earth.
Pegasus' mother was the daughter of Ocean's dangers—
            nature itself in the aspect of the snake-headed Medusa.
Pegasus was born when Medusa was beheaded
by the Greek prescription for orderly procession.[33]

Pegasus conveys the rattle of thunder & lightning through the skies
rides the condensation of evaporated ocean water
however   not now while Georgia O'Keeffe stands watch.
The northeast trades calming the sea around her
its high pressure discouraging the gait of low pressure
troughs & fronts from their northerly approach.

7

Canopy of Sky

Clearing the mind and sliding in
to that created space[34]

Georgia O'Keeffe—
passenger 27   age 51.   Her fine   articulated fingers
curl around the coarse dark wood of the upper deck.

Can a railing separate Georgia O'Keeffe
from Ocean Disc   &   Canopy of Sky?
Far removed from anywhere else

Five days at sea.

The *Lurline*   seafaring omphalos   Georgia O'Keeffe its axis mundi
like the erect mast of the upper deck   around which
Ocean Disc   &   Canopy of Sky revolve.
Axis of the radius   to a mobile edge   never reached.
Axis of the radius   to an edge she's left behind   like her past
        never quite disappears.
Axis of the radius   from which thought radiates.

This axis   Georgia O'Keeffe   is   *here.*

Whatever   beyond   is   *there.*

       unknown   foreign   other

riding Ocean's surface   its potential to become   known

       to be   *here.*

She has no idea what to call it

were she so inclined   she'd paint it.

Above the horizon   vertical is a mere protuberate—

two stacks of the *Lurline*

waves   swells   breaching whales   breaching dolphins   migratory birds.

Vertical is—

anywhere *up there*   the ceiling

      (even if *up there* is more horizontal than vertical).

Ceiling   from the Latin word *caelum*   means "sky."

From where she stands on the upper deck axis

she's no formula to measure distance to sky.

Five days at sea.

She muses at   sunrise   midday   sunset:

      Where am I?

Her external reference   integral to her internal identity

to her sense of security.

Her external *where she is*   integral to   her internal *who she is.*[35]

Her query more existential than the reference she seeks

her location by latitude   &   longitude
her location relative to north   south   east   west.

Like the desert beyond Taos
where she'd hunt
        for the sense of herself out there
        for the sense of life she feels
        to lie out in the sun naked[36]
where rock ridges & outcrops are like her ribs
river valleys like her blood vessels
hot winds like her breath.[37]

To identify   orient   &   measure inside Georgia O'Keeffe
is to identify   orient   &   measure outside landscape.
She'd paint the expansive landscape as Georgia O'Keeffe
as landscape would paint the expansive Georgia O'Keeffe.

        Who she is   as   where she is.

        I just feel so like expanding here—way out to the horizon—
        and up into the sunshine—and out into the night—
        I must be what is here now—[38]

Not inclined to view Georgia O'Keeffe distinct from landscape
to define a boundary between Georgia O'Keeffe & landscape
to define where she might begin   &   landscape might end
so twined are they.   To Georgia O'Keeffe
landscape *out there* is none other   than Georgia O'Keeffe *in here.*

She speaks to landscape as if speaking to herself:

How far might I stretch my heart?

Where might Georgia O'Keeffe end & Canopy of Sky   begin?
Is there a boundary between Georgia O'Keeffe & Canopy of Sky
is there a boundary between   Canopy of Sky & Space
    between *close to here* & *far out there*
    between troposphere &   stratosphere
    between exosphere & beyond?

Musing:
Do waves of light & sound reverberate within me
as they do among filaments of the universe
formed in the fever of the Big Bang
13.8 million years ago connecting the infinite array
of heavenly bodies as one?

Five days at sea.

Except for the horizontal motion of the ship
plowing through the sustained cadence of rolling swells
    —the crew calls this "forward"—
only stars & constellations offer a hint of direction.
On this warm Pacific marine night
those pixels of light   her most intimate counselors
guide her to reference points—the cardinal directions—
north   east   south   west.   The intermediate directions—

northeast   southeast   southwest   northwest
helping her locate *who she is*   &   *where she is*
in a particular place that otherwise defies placement.

Polaris
tip of the Little Dipper's handle
located about the north celestial pole   the North Star
the center around which the entire northern sky turns—
north on the compass.

Southern Cross
now slips below the horizon
visible before dawn during winter months till mid-January
with the perpendicular line that intersects it
with a point halfway between Alpha & Beta Centauri—
south on the compass.

Orion
southern sentinel of the northern hemisphere
Sirius   its canine companion.
Capella glows yellow like the sun in Auriga   the charioteer.
The misty ice blue cluster of the Pleiades
       shoulder of Taurus   the bull.

How to measure altitude   vertical distances to her celestial counselors
      distance measured as miles   or   distance as time?
How long does it take for light to make the journey to her eyes?
How many light-years?

(at 186,000 miles each earth-second).

(at 6,000,000,000,000 miles each earth-year).

from sun's warming light

8.3-minutes-old light.

from Proxima Centauri in the Southern Cross

4.24-years-old light

from Polaris

320-years-old light.

On its journey to Georgia O'Keeffe   gravity warps the light
the 8.3-minutes-old light
the 4.24-years-old light
the 320-years-old light
the light of her celestial counselors
appearing farther than they are—

it's uncanny seeing the heavenly bodies as they were eons ago.

The exterior spectacle helps the intimate grandeur unfold.[39]

However   she does not deign to paint   Canopy of Sky.

Feeling small in   Canopy of Sky   is not for Georgia O'Keeffe
neither is bewilderment   nightmare   nor vertigo.
She doesn't quiver from exposure to expanse   doesn't feel like
an insignificant collection of thoughts & body parts
making way through expanse as an insignificant being
engaged in an insignificant assignment
accumulating insignificant years of insignificant life

on a relatively insignificant planet
of the universe.[40]

Engaging with   Canopy of Sky   can be impossible to compute.
When engaging with the sky is too much to bear
        others look to the horizon
when engaging with the horizon is too much to bear
        they look to   Ocean Disc
when engaging with   Ocean Disc   is too much to bear
        they look for mammals or waves
        fish or birds   land   anything   out there.
If no mammals or waves   fish or birds   land   anything   out there
        no chatter that clutters   no obstacles that impede
        no passers-by   no one to attract   no one to repulse or ignore
they harness ways to fill the sky with stuff   time with activity
        &   mind with thought   to harness
        a semblance of certainty   familiarity   materiality   tangibility
        the presence of   "out there"   to affirm   assent   &   assure
        a presence of   "in here."

To assert   *me*   distinct from   *thee.*

On the other hand
when asserting *me* distinct from *thee*
        is too much to bear
when filling space with stuff   time with activity   &   mind with thought
        is too much to bear

when cluttering chatter   impeding obstacles   waves & mammals
fish & birds   land   objects   anything   *out there*
          is too much to bear
when   Ocean Disc   is too much to bear
when the horizon   is too much to bear
Georgia O'Keeffe   unlike others   unreservedly
engages with   Canopy of Sky

          its MAGNITUDE   its FULLNESS   its FREEDOM.

Were she to paint Canopy of Sky
she'd paint the simultaneous revelation of a one-second-old yesterday
with a 13.8-billion-years-old yesterday
past cosmic events as if today
today's cosmic events as tomorrow
the collapse of the accepted sequence of
past   present   future.
The further away the light   the older it is
moving faster   bodies and energies expand the universe
as Einstein postulated.

          The poetry that moves me most is the poetry of infinity—
          where things are lost in each other and limits vanish.[41]

Were she to paint Canopy of Sky
she'd paint the spirit of the lemniscate
the figure eight that flows back on itself
like the Ouroboros   the snake that eats its tail—

the continuing cycle of birth   life   death
having no timely dimension.

She'd paint endless shape & endless color
like her gyrating musical notes of 20 years before[42]
or   *Abstraction Blue 1927.*

She'd paint infinite possibility   invitation   arousal
          seduction   intrigue   inviting—
sparks of yawning deep magentas
tinted sparks of gradual unfolding
tempting whites & pinks
guiding dark indigo undulations
seducing excitement of anticipation   &   almost   but not quite
revealing hints of unknown shapes   colors   smells   tastes
she'd paint the sequence   moment by moment   by itself
uncontainably erotic—life itself.
Like James Hillman's "beauty"—the operations of nature
essence of artistic creation
          not adornment   not decoration   not transcending.[43]

Then turning to her critics   she'd succinctly say:

          If you simply drop your incessant infantile preoccupation
          with genitalia   &   take the time   you'll see
          as simply as inhaling & exhaling—
          I merely paint LIFE.

Although the previous night's new moon
orbiting more or less 250,000 miles from earth
partially blocked the sun's light   roughly 93,000,000 miles away
in Georgia O'Keeffe's world   these distances are meaningless
        curiously   what matters
is that the sun's diameter is about 400 times larger
than the moon's diameter   &   the sun's distance to earth is roughly
400 times farther than the moon
so that sun & moon appear in the sky as roughly the same size
like fraternal twins hovering above her front yard.

Were she to paint Canopy of Sky
she'd paint a celebration
she'd the sky with the moon
she'd paint the sky with a flat white cloud
she'd paint the sky above the clouds.[44]

Yet   she paints nothing.

Five days at sea.

Marks no time at all
engagement with a two-dimensional passage
through a *present* of no thickness
time between   *once was*   &   *is coming*
a   *present*   that she cannot seem to reach.
The closer she seems to   *present*
the farther & faster   *present*   recedes.

That elusive *present*
available to but a few
transforms   before she knows   into   *then.*
The moment of   *present*   here & now
has already passed before it can be recognized.
Unable to be *present* in the present
how can progress be measured?

Sky reveals   *past*   heavenly bodies as they were.
Horizon presents   *present*   never to be reached.
Ocean holds   *future*   whose waves ache to appear.

It's nothing she can measure
nothing she can comprehend.   Compared to this
all else can seem mundane.

The constant blow of the salty air & sway of the ship.

8

What Is It About Space?

*There is just nothing out there—the quiet and bigness of it—and
what I see seems more like music than anything I ever saw—a
marvelously round trembling living thing—wonderful sky—
wonderful jewel—so much of it out here—you have never seen
SKY—loving it more than ever it seems—anything that makes you
feel quiet and bigness like that is marvelous.[45]*

What is it   about Space   that makes her feel so alive?
     Calmly caresses?
     Showers her with boundless freedom   infinite possibility?
     Makes her *EXPLODE* with orgasmic euphoria?

What is it   about Space   that undermines grief?
     Washes tears   clears despair   heals the hurt?
     Helps dissolve the belligerent cacophony of
     negative emotions & perverse thoughts?

As an artist   how can she not know what Space   is
     &   what it is not
     &   the mechanism by which Space enriches the profound   &
         everyday ways
            of thoughts   &   doings?

As her point of departure   she thanks Isaac Newton   his Scholium
his two allusions to Space—

      Relative Space—of discernable size   shape   measurement
      Absolute Space—invisible   infinite & eternal   Spirit[46]

Of Relative Space   the Space of *who she is*   &   *where she is*
the Space of her inner   &   outer wilds   the Space
with which she generally works—

Space #1
One of five operations of nature
the container enabling the other four operations of
earth   water   fire   &   wind   to engage

Space #2
Natural complement of form
     Space   containing form   &   contained by form
     Space   containing sound   &   contained by sound
     Space   containing thought   &   contained by thought
     Space   containing time   &   contained by time
     Space   containing words   numbers   characters   &
        contained by words   numbers   characters

Space #3
Arena   for the interactive performance of things & thoughts
in expressive & erotic patterns of motion & rest
     with this Space   anything is possible
    without this Space   nothing is possible

no place in which to be   no place to which to go

no one with whom to be   no one with whom to go

Space #4

Interstices of hydrogen filaments spanning the universe—

Space of the cosmic web of threaded gaseous structures

weaving together the galaxies & solar systems formed

in the fever of the Big Bang 13.8 billion years ago.

The natural poetry of Einstein & Heisenberg's

unimaginable relatively uncertain expanse.

Black energy   black matter   black holes

massive young galaxies creating

disturbances in the Big Bang

theory of origins.[47]

Unbound wonder & reverence.

> *And suddenly, Neruda, he sees*
> *the heavens*
> *unfastened*
> *and open,*
> *planets,*
> *palpitating plantations,*
> *the darkness perforated,*
> *riddled*
> *with arrows, fire, and flowers,*
> *the overpowering night, the universe.*[48]

For the sense of herself out there
for the sense of life she feels.

Of Absolute Space   of Spirit
in which   engaging with Space   is to behold silence

                    beholding silence   is to engage inner luminosity.

She engages Anaximander of Miletus
his 2,600-odd-years-ago search for the genesis of things & thought
eschews Hesiod's Space of supreme sky gods   thunder gods
lightning gods   storm gods   wind gods
eschews the traditional ideas of divinity   &   delegates
the revered role of the gods
to the *apeiron*   "the boundless."
  Space
  as the first principle of being
  surrounding all & steering all
  neither metaphysical   nor   transcendent

  rather   natural   real   here   now
  incorruptible   indestructible   inexhaustible
  immortal   infinite.[49]
  Space as Divinity.

She engages Plato
his 2,400-odd-years-ago search for the genesis of things & thought
he invokes three natures—

one   generation   an intelligible pattern always the same
        invisible   imperceptible by any sense   granted alone to Divinity
two   imitation of the generation   a created copy of the intelligible
        arising   abiding   dissolving   perceived by the senses
three   Space   in which generation takes place
        nurse   receptacle   container of all created copies.

Plato's Space
        cannot be sensed
        has no place in heaven or earth
        yet is always present   apprehended as a dream
        &
        never   in any way   assumes the shape of things it contains
        &   unchanged   never changes its nature.[50]
        Space as Divinity.

She engages Aurelius Augustine
erudite scholar & student of Plato & Plotinus
his 1,600-odd-years-ago search for the genesis of things & thought
per his *Confessions*   he invokes a Trinity
a metamorphic mutation of Plato's three natures—
one   from Plato's divine ideal   Father   of God
two   from Plato's created copy   Son   of God
        & through revelations into the infinite breath of life
three   from Plato's Space   the Holy Spirit *(pneuma)*
        the natural boundless rhythm of the exoteric & esoteric
                arising   abiding   dissolving
        enabling things & thoughts of the profound & everyday

a *where*   in which to become[51]

Space as Divinity.

Space   said William Blake   *is a state of mind.*[52]

She engages the three Buddhist Vehicles—
   Foundation   Perfection   Fruition.[53]
In Pali & Sanskrit   Space means   "mere lack of obstruction."
among the unchanged & unconditioned—
liberation *(nirvāṇa)*   non-inherence *(shūnyatā)*   Space *(ākāśa)*
are equivalent.

The three Buddhist Vehicles say:
Beholding *nirvāṇa & shūnyatā*   is like beholding Space.
Beholding Space   is like beholding *nirvāṇa & shūnyatā.*
Beholding Space   is Space-like realization.
Beholding Space   is the Space-like mind.
Space-like absorption   is the womb of Awakening.
Space-like absorption   is the womb of luminosity & knowing.
Space-like absorption   is the secret womb of teachings.
Space-like absorption   is the fruit of practice.

The three Buddhist Vehicles say Space is—
   not an   *it   thing   this   that*
  not physical   not metaphysical
  not visible   not measurable
  not produced   not extinguished
  not temporary   not perishable

  does not obstruct things & thought

is not obstructed by things & thought.

The three Buddhist Vehicles also say Space is—
> without ego
> without affliction
> without discrimination
> without want & don't want
> without envy   anger   jealousy   hatred   malice   pride.

As such
The body is like Space.
The mind   is like Space.
All appearances   are like Space.
All thoughts & things   are like Space.
The perfections of place   are like Space.
All outer   inner   secret landscapes   are like Space.
All vision sound smell taste things thoughts are like Space.
Relief from afflictive emotions   is like Space.
Relief from pain & panic   is like Space.
Relief from loss   is like Space.[54]

The great Bodhisattvas asked:
Where dwell the diamonds of Body   Speech   &   Mind?
> Buddhas replied: The diamonds dwell in Space.
> The Bodhisattvas then asked: Where dwells Space?
> And the Buddhas replied: Nowhere!
Then those Bodhisattvas in wonderment & amazement
became silent.[55]

Space   by its nature   is fundamentally unknowable
Hearing Rilke:

The space within us reaches out, translates each thing.[56]

Five days at sea.
Georgia O'Keeffe   51 years old
first-class passenger 27   on the SS *Lurline*
the coarse dark wood railing around which
she curls her fine articulated fingers
cannot separate Georgia O'Keeffe from Space.

What happens out there—far—far away?
Removed from elsewhere
sailing a strange world.
Hawai'i just might be the kind of place   being even farther
that will offer a remarkably satisfying experience
        pineapples notwithstanding.[57]

II

WATERFALLS

9

Haleakalā

—I will be off in the far away—[58]

Friday, March 10—Quizzically, Georgia O'Keeffe eyes the plane set to fly her from Honolulu's John Rodgers Airport to Maui, an Inter-Island Airways Sikorsky S-43 "Baby Clipper" amphibian. It makes no sense. The wheel well is positioned where the door should be, a floater device where the wheel should be. And there doesn't seem to be a door. She sees no way to board.   Like that recurring dream: *Must find a way inside ... train, bus, house, lover, however, the hole is plugged ... its getting late ... much stuff to carry.* Not to worry. Igor Sikorsky's carafe of cleverness had placed a rectangular hatch atop the fuselage like a surgeon's cut into its spine near the tail of the plane. The airport crew rolls a portable stairway over the tarmac to just below the hatch, directing passengers up to and inside the plane.

She descends the stairway into the plane's compressed belly. Walks briskly through the cabin to find her seat. This particular plane seats 11 passengers.   There are four single seats on the left and three pairs of seats followed by a single seat on the right. There's a center aisle between the two sides. Georgia O'Keeffe prefers to sit by herself. She takes the single seat in the back on the right. Were she to sit on the left, her hosts advised, she'd be disappointed, blinded by the morning sun, unable to see what she wished to see, unable to pick out the deep, vibrant greens and blues of the land and ocean.

Mr. Sikorsky's carafe of cleverness had also crafted this Inter-Island Airways Sikorsky S-43 "Baby Clipper" amphibian plane with a vertical strut to lift its 85-foot wing and pair of propeller engines above the fuselage to keep the engines dry during aquatic landing and takeoff. Lifting the wing offers Georgia O'Keeffe an unobstructed view of the sea below. The curvature of the Inter-Island Airways Sikorsky S-43 "Baby Clipper" wing is designed to fly into the wind, assuring sufficient lift and velocity during takeoff from water and remaining aloft as needed while landing. The flying boat's cruising altitude of 7,000 feet and 185 mph speed is sufficiently low and slow enough to allow her a survey of the scene below in greater detail.

Her quickening breath matches the sharply aroused pace of the aircraft; her heartbeat matches the two Pratt & Whitney R-1690-52 air-cooled radial piston engines accelerating over the tarmac, 750 horsepower for each thrusting engine, 750 beats of her thrusting heart. The moment of liftoff, wheels breaking contact yet still spinning, nose penetrating the sky. Her glans swells every time she takes-off, never fails.

Flying in the heart of the rainy season, she watches the aerial performance of clouds recompose each minute. Fortunately, this March 10th morning, the northeast winds skirt the south side of the islands, blowing them aside, exacting an exotic blue tropical sky.

Georgia O'Keeffe's plane flies east, turns south over the Kalaupapa

Peninsula of Moloka'i, then hangs high above the pineapple plantations and deep gorges of Lāna'i. Passing the immensely high sea cliffs, the plane swings toward the Maui coast into the prevailing northeast trade winds funneled over the Isthmus between Maui's two mountains, and into the Mā'alaea Airport near the south shore of the Isthmus.

Mā'alaea Airport had been condemned, actually, just the previous winter. Considered unsafe for the larger and newer aircraft being phased into use, the chief inspector of the Bureau of Air Commerce in Washington, DC, chose to write the airport off the books. When the new Maui airport at Pu'unēnē opens in three months, Mā'alaea will close permanently.

Were winds blowing from the south, ferrying the heavy winter storms, instead of from the northeast, Georgia O'Keeffe's Inter-Island Airways Sikorsky S-43 "Baby Clipper" amphibian plane would have flown around the northeast shore of the West Maui volcano into an impressively dramatic welcome.

She'd be amazed by all the geological sorts of goings on below—

She'd be amazed by the gyrating coves and ridges of the coastline. Vertical walls of hardened black lava, measuring thousands-of-feet cliff top to Pacific Ocean below. More than a million persistent years of basalt magma building up the island, waves pulverizing and wearing it away. More than a million persistent years of heavy tropical rains splitting blocks of basalt magma along its vertical fissures, earthquakes heaving them into the ocean, carving deep valleys.

She'd be amazed by the coastal blowholes like the geysers at Yellowstone, spitting explosive jets of water 50 feet into the sky, timed as if wash and rinse cycles intended to clean the air.

She'd be amazed by Kahakuloa Head, the massive volcanic dome of extremely dense pumice and cinder, like an erect 600-foot phallus rising from the edge of the ocean, a remnant of Maui's third series of volcanic bursts that bubbled out of the ground just about a million years ago. Its smaller dome-like partner, Puʻu Kahuliʻanapa, close by. It would remind her of Half Dome at Yosemite.

She'd be amazed by the water vapor, its condensing in the valleys and evaporating in the skies, hiding and revealing layers of basalt magma, donning its stash of secret personae.

She'd be amazed by Waiheʻe Valley, one of the mountain's four "Gateways to Heaven," cloaked with midmorning layers of beige and gray silky gauze clouds, carried there on its native wind called Kili-ʻoʻopu,[59] discreetly covering the valley cleavage.

And she'd be amazed by ʻĪao Valley, which she would possess as her own.

To a New Yorker, it could make no sense at all. To a New Yorker, it could be like *Lost Horizons* meets *The Wizard of Oz*. To a New Yorker, it could be more like a touch of burlesque. To a New Yorker, it could be like 42nd Street. Georgia O'Keeffe would shiver at the craziness of it all—a perplexing, wondrous kind of glee, delightfully wrapped into the volcanic landscape below—had she flown around Maui's northeast shore, had she flown into the airport from the north into the southerly winter winds rather than from the south into the northeast winds.

Far away in another world here—(down below) the lava makes a cra-
zy coast—black with the bright blue sea—pounding surf rising very
high in the air in many places—queer formations worn in the lava—
bridges—gate ways—holes through it where it seems solid where the
water comes up in spray—hissing and blowing—[60]

Georgia O'Keeffe disembarks the plane at Māʻalaea Airport on the south shore of the Isthmus. It's just before nine. She's about to descend to the tarmac. The sniff of fresh morning musk, rich volcanic soil, a sweet succulent scent.

She hesitates at the top of the stairs. Stares at the raw volcanic mountain shield they call Haleakalā, offspring of Earth and Sky. Haleakalā: "House of the Sun." Haleakalā: Sacred center of the island, where Maui held ground and restrained the sun's movement so the island would benefit from longer daylight, which perhaps explains Maui's migration westerly and northerly on the Pacific Plate. Haleakalā: Realm of divinity, were she inclined to such belief. No matter. Haleakalā doesn't seek Georgia O'Keeffe's approval.

Haleakalā had last erupted in 1790 CE, a mere dozen years after the arrival of British explorer Captain James Cook, perhaps a sign of the volcano's unhappiness with the introduction of foreign pestilence and disease brought by his crew.

From where she stands above the tarmac, Georgia O'Keeffe doesn't see the volcano's northeast, east and south slopes, where ocean waves and rains carried by the northeast trade winds have chiseled hundreds of thousands of years of spectacular, deeply dissected ridges and canyons.

Nor does she see the shield's peak of almost fresh cinder, nor the dry alpine desert.

However, from where she stands above the tarmac, Georgia O'Keeffe does see the volcano's concave western slope, a relatively smooth terrain rising 10,000 feet into the sky, less eroded by wind and rain than its other sides.

From where she stands above the tarmac, Georgia O'Keeffe sees nothing in Haleakalā's western slope that resembles the vitality and vibrancy of those undulating serpent-like landforms, nothing referencing the esoteric landscapes inspired or discovered by divination or dowsing. She sees nothing in Haleakalā's topography blatantly looking like private body parts engaging her with sensual charge.

There's nothing akin to the erotic play of her New Mexico mesas rising above storm-carved arroyos, nothing akin to her Pedernal and Abiquiú Lake, nothing akin to those extinct volcanic cones rising from the level desert plains. There's nothing sexually explicit like Kahakuloa's two protruding phalluses; nothing like the familiar heads and foreskins of Tent Rocks near Santa Fe; nothing like Canyon de Chelly's Spider Rock, the 800-dignified-foot red sandstone spire protruding into the sky, home of the Diné's Spider Woman.

She sees no V-shaped valleys like her New Mexico *Black Place*, her (soon-to-be-painted) *Ghost Ranch Waterfall*, nor the shrub-surrounded orifice like Carrizo Plain's Painted Rock in central California, nor a landscape of full, prominent breasts like Scotland's Paps of Jura and Ireland's Paps of Dana.

Georgia O'Keeffe sees nothing extraordinary about the west slope of Haleakalā. Yet she senses something curious about the gentle concavity of the slope. The intimate way it seems to cup the air in the geometry of its simple parabolic curve, the tender dialogue between Earth and Sky. The geometry that produces the pressure differential that invites the strong, cold northwesterly wind called Kiu of Haleakalā[61] to fly onto the mountain and reside there. She visualizes the wind gradually roll down the mountain directly to where she stands above the tarmac, perambulating around her more than once and then wrapping itself around her neck like a garland. A wreath made of wind. Curious, yet also somewhat familiar. She'd felt something like it at Ghost Ranch, an intimacy between her and the mesa. The arousal of giving and receiving.

From where she stands above the tarmac, Georgia O'Keeffe wonders what Haleakalā intends to reveal to her. What it might bestow in its geology. In its shape. In its stories. In its raw, everyday nakedness. She's smitten, and not sure why.

Perhaps Haleakalā is tasting her, testing her, seeing what she's made of before swallowing and transporting her into its core. If Georgia O'Keeffe looks for approval, to be granted the opportunity for adventure, perhaps Haleakalā requires an equivalent exchange before bestowing its treasures, and before advising Maui to accept her.

Hesitating at the top of the stairs in that singular span of time, who knows how long, she considers if her engagement with the mountain is to be at all similar to Rilke's exchange with landscape:

Earth, isn't this what you want? To arise in us, invisible?
Is it not your dream, to enter us wholly
there's nothing left outside us to see?
What, if not transformation
is your deepest purpose? [62]

Hesitating at the top of the stairs in that singular span of time, who knows how long, she wonders to what degree Haleakalā's arising, abiding and dissolving will be woven with her own libido, to what degree this Maui landscape, as with her beloved New Mexico, will begin weaving through the interstices of who she is. As she makes her way into this new landscape, she wonders if their engagement will be as William Blake might suggest:

Saying
'Each grain of Sand,
Every Stone of the Land,
Each rock & each hill,
Each fountain & rill,
Each herb & each tree,
Mountain, hill, earth & sea,
Cloud, Meteor & Star,
Is Georgia O'Keeffe seen Afar. [63]

Hesitating at the top of the stairs in that singular span of time, who knows how long, she wonders if she'll be privy to the layers of landscape that she's heard elders call *kaona,* the layered fruits of Hawai'i:

As Earth Mother Papahānaumoku and Sky Father Wākea consummated, they produced everything in the cosmos; and everything in the cosmos was alive: the ocean and the wind and the sacred land they call ʻĀina. And this mountain Haleakalā was the product of their love. And in accepting this love, people would agree to abide in harmonious intimacy with everything in the Maui cosmos.[64]

She hears from the tarmac:

Madam, other passengers wish to disembark!

Smitten, the morning's sweet sweep of life.

And she's barely left the aircraft.

10

Meeting 'Īao Valley

—This island seems to be drifting off
in space some place I've never been—[65]

Friday, March 10—Harold Stein, director of the Boy Scouts of Maui, greets Georgia O'Keeffe inside the terminal building. Harold is a family friend of Willis Jennings, plantation manager of the Kaʻelekū Sugar Company, and will take her later in the day to stay at the Jennings' residence on the far east side of the island near Hāna, on the east slopes of Haleakalā.

Before driving to Hāna, Harold will introduce Georgia O'Keeffe to 'Īao Valley. He believes they'll find a mutual respect, if not a kindred spirit, in each other's company. As Harold wishes theirs to be a direct face-to-face introduction, he'll approach the valley straight on, rather than by an oblique, surreptitious snake from the side along the more direct northerly Honoapiʻilani Highway, straddling the eastern base of Mauna Kahālāwai (ascribed by those from elsewhere with the unpoetic name of the West Maui Mountains).

Leaving the airport, Harold turns from Mauna Kahālāwai and heads northeast onto Dairy Road (now Kūihelani Highway) toward the center of the Isthmus, the saddle connecting Maui's two mountains.

Georgia O'Keeffe barely pays attention to Harold. She responds simply, though cordially, to his attempts at conversation. Absorbed with the scent and shape of Haleakalā, floating in the morning's clear, pale blue sky, she barely notices through Harold's window the deep, wet, leafy cliffs of Waikapū Valley, the steep ridges and canyons like huge interlacing fingers, and the stream that continues to carve them, weaving back and forth. Eighteen thousand years ago, when the sea was 400 feet lower, the stream flowed north and entered the ocean at Kahului Bay, where they're now heading. Subsequently, hardened sand dunes blocked the stream's northerly route, forcing it to flow south into Māʻalaea Bay, near the airport where she landed. The rich genealogical history of Maui streams.[66]

She barely notices through Harold's window that clear skies south of the island don't preclude the approach of weather systems from the east. She barely notices the clouds outlined in blush pink riding on saddles of the northeast trade winds descending onto the mountain, blatantly covering the canyon cliffs on the right side of the valley, while a singular white cloud tartly hangs above the slopes on the left. She barely notices through Harold's window the sheer sheets of gray, wet with rain. The island's seemingly capricious climatic variables are unfamiliar to Georgia O'Keeffe. To the island, they make perfect sense.

It takes just a few minutes to drive to Kahului. A right turn at the main intersection directs them to the Hāna Highway, and the estate of her host. Too early in the day to head directly to Hāna, Harold turns left towards the Maui Grand Hotel in Wailuku, where he currently resides. Immediately, they face the most daunting, deliciously deep green valley Georgia O'Keeffe has ever seen. It strikes her that this valley's enveloping "female" is the equivalent of Yosemite Valley's striking "male."

Harold parks on the shoulder of the road. Emerging from the car, Harold says:

Georgia O'Keeffe, I'd like you to meet our ʻĪao Valley—
the "Valley of Supreme Clouds." Valley, this here is Georgia O'Keeffe.

At the precise moment Georgia O'Keeffe is introduced to ʻĪao Valley, from the line on the compass marked 60 degrees east, from a point 40 miles behind them, the younger Haleakalā captures the sun from the clasp of the clouds. The shaft of sunlight a mere infant, Haleakalā sorts it into its constituent prismatic colors: purple—blue—green—yellow—orange—red—and gifts the shaft of light to Mauna Kahālāwai, its older sister by a half million years.

The shaft of light is directed to Halekiʻi-Pihana Heiau. Once the main temple of Mauna Kahālāwai, Halekiʻi-Pihana Heiau reigned from the solidified sand dune deposited during one interglacial period onto the north shoulder of the valley high above ʻĪao Stream. Its doors facing the direction of the rising summer solstice sun, the temple mediated between the valley's opening and the Pacific Ocean. The temple gathers the light and gifts it to Georgia O'Keeffe.

Georgia O'Keeffe stares at the valley as veins of bright, chromatic brushes of light deftly caress the temple grounds, sand dunes, valley slopes and steep cliffs with iridescent key lime yellows and 200-watt greens, the same colors she used for *Pink Moon and Blue Lines, 1923*. Light colored copper and rust etch the million-year-old ridges flanking the left cliffs of the valley, before gradually migrating to the right. For the briefest of seconds, colors deeply intensify before they silently absorb into the mantle of mauve grays of approaching clouds beginning to cloak the valley.

A light containing within it the full frame of time: a gift that's traveled eight minutes and 18 seconds, more or less, from the past, a finger of immanent brilliance right here and right now, the potential for intoxicating nourishment with insights she's about to discover. She excitedly observes:

> *Notwithstanding the extraordinary sunrises I've seen in Texas and my New Mexico desert, the muted sky of the pre-dawn, the expanding glow emerging over the horizon from behind a sprinkle of crisp clouds, shafts of light appearing and disappearing and the kind of halo effects. Sister, never seen anything like it!*[67]

She forgets to breathe.

Haleakalā sends no light into the valley orifice. Except for a faint reflection of iridescence on the tips of clouds hovering just inside, a glance of light narrowly silhouettes an outline of the valley lips.

Nor is light cast on Wailuku River (the other name of ʻĪao Stream), its life-affirming waters unceremoniously diverted into a system of ditches by the Wailuku Sugar Company in 1881, sending millions of gallons of water each day to irrigate the company's vast hungry fields of sugarcane plantations, the diversion compromising the traditional and cultural significance of the stream, the natural sacred flow of the waters disregarded. A sacrilege.[68]

(And in 1981, the natural flow of the Wailuku River will be further usurped, artlessly commanded by the US Army Corps of Engineers into a debris basin, diversion levees leading from both sides of the river, and channelized through a 3,500-foot-long cage of reinforced concrete. The massive quantities of water from frequent cloudbursts and downpours that otherwise would naturally scour banks and deposit sand, gravel, rocks and boulders instead will be imprisoned within these walls enabling lands of the natural floodplain to be covered with townhouses, industrial park warehouses and parking for freight and container depots.[69] However, when the water level exceeds the designed capacity of the concrete channel, the stream will surmount the concrete walls, overflow its banks and leave in its wake the river's scoured, saturated, washed, broken, torn and cast-off detritus).

No, Haleakalā doesn't cast light on this section of 'Īao Stream-Wailuku River.

Nor does Haleakalā cast light on Paukūkalo Beach at Nehe Point, (near the end of the concrete ditch constructed 42 years later, unceremoniously altering the character of this place, as well), where rapid flowing waters of the mountain would converge with waves and tides of the Pacific, the dramatic change in velocity causing the river to unload its cargo of sand, gravel and stones from upstream and here construct the delta made of the deposited materials. This landscape, where the waters meet, is considered sacred, transactional grounds for spiritual renewal.

The river also unloads at these sacred, transactional grounds an unwarranted, irreverent burden of solid artifacts and liquid pollutants, dumped and poured upstream with disregard and disrespect into the waters and carried down toward the ocean, where the Pacific unceremoniously transports the solids elsewhere along the beach or farther away, who knows where, and dilutes and chemically reconstitutes the density and potency of the liquid effluents, taking who knows how long. The pathetic legacy of people's incomprehensible relationship with the land, waters and sky.

However ephemeral, something is inexplicably real about the light cast from Haleakalā she's witnessed. A reality that contrasts with the airport, roads, buildings and ways of living that people not from here seem to inhabit. She thinks of the event not at all as mystical or miraculous, neither extraterrestrial nor supernatural, neither transcendent nor the emanation of a heavenly spirit. Not a believer in dogma posed by religious orders, she's witnessed a natural and earthly aesthetic of spiritual dimensions:

> Unbound wonder and reverence—
> naked—in silence and the unbearable lightness of space.
> Beauty and divinity, arising together in the same breath.

This fiesta of light takes but a singular span of time. Dark clouds begin veiling the mountain. Mauna Kahālāwai isn't ready to invite Georgia O'Keeffe. Following her 10-days in Hāna, she'll return to this Valley of Supreme Clouds.

The morning's sweet sweep of life.

11
Entering ʻĪao Valley

Tuesday March 21—Georgia O'Keeffe steps onto the semicircular driveway at the entrance to the Maui Grand Hotel. Constructed in 1916 at the southeast corner of Church and Main in the city of Wailuku at elevation 300 feet above sea level at the base of ʻĪao Valley on the slope of Mauna Kahālāwai, the two-story hotel faces east, its spacious lobby, courtyard and second floor lanai providing a sense of its luxury.

Willis has driven Georgia O'Keeffe to the hotel, where she'll stay for her remaining week in Maui. His 12-year-old daughter, Patricia will be her companion and guide for the next two days before returning with her dad to Hāna. Although Willis has kindly rented a Chevrolet station wagon for Georgia O'Keeffe to use to explore this part of the island, she stands there scowling at the car. How is she to drive this ancient three-on-the-floor gear shift? She's told there are no modern column-shift models available. Uncertain about her proficiency, she's encouraged by Patricia. All right. Turning left from the driveway onto Main Street, she drives directly toward the valley.

Main Street climbs slightly for three quarters of a mile, past pineapple fields on the left and a small community of several houses on the right. The road splits at the mouth of the valley. Alu Road breaks left toward a farm (In the future, the farm will be sold to land developers who will transform the fields into a suburb called Wailuku Heights). She veers right down a narrow, winding, precipitous dirt lane into the valley. ʻĪao Valley Road.

Constructed in 1906, the road seems no more advanced than the path it supposedly replaced, a narrow, horizontal shelf excavated into the side of the mountain. On the left, the valley cliffs rise almost vertically. She quickly averts her eyes from the cliffs and looks down the steep slopes through the trees to the river somewhere below on the right before focusing back on the road. No guardrails to keep her from sliding off the side of the road to that dark somewhere below. Contained by the lush forest, only an occasional sporadic house now edges the road. For the most part, she feels embraced by the forest, as she slowly motors through the irregularly shaped, moist, misty cylinder of dense canopy. Forest and air are heavy with the thick residue of frequent heavy rains. The ground here has to absorb no less than 100 inches a year of rainwater; otherwise, the unstable slopes of saturated soil and rock will slump and flow down to the valley bottom like a viscous fluid, adding more debris to the flooding stream. In the caldera, the ancient center of the volcanic mountain to which ʻĪao Valley Road is heading, there will be three to four times as much rain.

The road is so narrow, a truck would have to stop, reverse and reconfigure its trajectory so it can slither around the crooked curves. When vehicles meet from opposite directions, one has to veer onto the slip of a shoulder to allow the other to pass. She dares not execute such a maneuver.

Frankly, Georgia O'Keeffe is scared. With Patricia in the passenger seat, she won't exceed her self-imposed 10-mile-per-hour speed. Unable to see very far beyond the edge of the road, she doesn't see anyplace she'd want to paint. Even so, it's too dangerous anywhere along this confined, forsaken road to stop. So smitten by the promise of the valley's potential, however, she sets her fear aside and continues to drive.

After what seemingly feels like an entire hour to drive the mile and a quarter, the tunnel curls open. They come to a level clearing, where an open meadow beside the road, elevation 680 feet, is wide enough for her to pull over without falling off the edge or blocking other vehicles. She exhales, relieved after the harrowing drive.

Emerging from the car, Georgia O'Keeffe is given no time to prepare for the gift the valley immediately offers to her. The glory of this majestic, deep-green valley. The sublimity of unadulterated bliss, the full measure of sensory pleasure gladdening every pore of her body, every one of her organs, her lungs, her heart, her belly. Absorbing the entirety of the valley, she feels like she's about to explode!

The spectacle of vertical green and rocky cliffs on each side of the valley soaring thousands of feet, who knows how high. Cliffs penetrating billowing tropical clouds, spacious sky cloaking the green cliffs. No way to tell where earth ends and sky begins.

The continuous corrugation of cliffs of volcanic proportions: ridge and canyon, ridge and canyon. Deep, dark, wet canyons like the inner folds of an accordion alternating with outer folds of bright, dry, extruding vertical ridges. The geomorphic play of concave space alternating with convex form. The oscillating pattern of light and shade gracing valley cliffs like a ballerina's hands would caress those of her partner. Palms out, palms hidden, forward and back, up and down: a ballet of arising, abiding and dissolving.

The idea that music could be translated into something for the eye.[70]

Each canyon is the collective signature of a million years of celestial, geological and tropical authorship. A million-year engagement between the forces of magma's arising and abiding, and the forces of weathering that impel it to dissolve. Into layers of basalt magma that build up the mountain, wind and rain continue to drive, pound and dig; chisel, carve and hammer; break, shear and tear, while roots of trees, shrubs and ground cover furrow and grow within weakening joints of the rock.

Deep, well-defined, green canyons of soaring cliffs. Deep recesses, who knows how deep, sculpted into the valley's cliffs. Blocks of rock pulled from cliff walls, heaved onto canyon floors covered by the rock creep and rock slide, detritus piled up as talus, slopes worn down and leveled as high terraces. The detritus transported by tributary waters of each canyon toward its mouth, detritus carried farther into ʻĪao Stream, scouring the valley bed with its scraping sand, gravel, boulders.

Where the talus slopes are not as precipitous, where rain and low vegetative growth have broken the rock down into soil, habitat is provided for the thickets of trees and shrubs and the insect and animals that abide there. Each canyon's ecological brood of plant, insect and animal species and genera is unique to its particular ecological landscape, discouraged from cross-pollinating and interbreeding with those of neighboring canyons.[71]

The spectacle of clouds dashing and deftly draping shoulders of recessed canyons, exposed rock outcrops supporting shelves of rich tropical trees and shrubs, streams washing hidden canyons with reservoirs of rainwater, and waterfalls plunging through thick tropical forests. Birds flying about, their sweet choral dialogues enticing potential partners.

The spectacle of all those shades and shadows and tones of green greens; greens that make the Lake Placid landscapes she'd painted look pallid: peacock greens, olive greens, grass greens, kelp greens—Prismacolor 907, 911, 913, 1090 greens.

The valley hushes the wind to silence, and Georgia O'Keeffe, standing immobilized, is drawn to the syncopated staccato of white water cataracts just upstream, the stream tunneling under the house-sized boulders that sometime in the past were blocks of basalt that sheared from the ridges above as landslides, free-falling down cliffs and tumbling through the valley floor into the stream to be transported as easily as the lighter gravel and stones the stream also rolled, bounced and carried. Finally at rest, the boulders would be scraped, scoured, smoothed and made spherical by the pounding force of rain and the stream's natural wearing.

She hears the subdued sighs of ʻĪao Stream weaving through the far side of the meadow into banks and sweeping around gravel bars. Flowing there across the more level valley floor, its velocity greatly diminished, it begins to meander, something that streams naturally do to equalize their release of energy between the steeper convexity of the stream bed upstream and the more level concavity down below. Geomorphologists call it the principle of least work. With its reduced velocity, the stream is unable to carry the load of heavy rocks it acquired upstream, and drops it, creating the broad alluvial terrace that extends from the far side of the slope to the meadow on which Georgia O'Keeffe stands immobilized.

The smell of mist-covered banks; heavy air foaming with scents of broad, moist overhanging leaves.

(Seventy-nine years later, the field is secured with a chain-link fence. A layer of heavy fabric covers the fence, segmenting the view. Under a mature mango tree on the field, a table with a gallon jug of water. Two uninhabited trailers are parked there, too. All inhabitants and dwellings that occupied the meadow after Georgia O'Keeffe stands here are gone, washed away by the stream that continually floods the valley; the latest flood, 18 months prior, caused the road to be closed).

A wood trestle bridge crosses the river ahead. Near the bridge, a large boulder with a bronze plaque commemorates the events that took place here. In front, a wooden pole supports a thin wooden man wearing a long black coat. He points to the right and underneath, a white sign with the word Kepaniwai.

Georgia O'Keeffe's eyes are drawn across the valley to the V-shaped canyon opening from the cliff wall there on the right. Like other canyons in the valley, this has been carved by a million annual cycles of rain, wind and water—enlarged, deepened and bisected by the water rushing through it.

In the center of the canyon, midway from the top, a waterfall spills through a ridge and over a crevasse. Cliffs of basalt soar precipitously, with deep, dark, wet gullies, many hidden from view, bifurcating the rock faces on all sides. The exclamation in the middle of the canyon, its brazen corporality captures her like that of the sun's instantaneous point of light at the horizon. She internalizes the ecological encounters between forces of nature that build and the forces of nature that erode as if they were the operations of her own body. She finds herself in this liminal landscape at this liminal moment as between darkness and light, between the search and the found, between slumber and awakening. Of course!

Figure 1. Naoki Kutsunai, *The Canyon*, 1937.

And she notes to herself: *I must paint this!*[72]

About to engage in a many-splendored encounter, Georgia O'Keeffe doesn't allow the tenor of her voice betray her intimate affection for the canyon and the waterfall as she calmly says to Patricia: *This looks like a good place. Can you keep yourself busy for a bit?* Patricia nods and finds a place by a tree to sit. Eyeing some guavas across the river, she thinks to go pick them, decides better not, wishing to avoid the wrath of her guest, the likes of which she endured near Hāna the previous week when she disappeared for a longer period of time than Georgia O'Keeffe thought safe.

Georgia O'Keeffe sets up her easel on the level ground a few feet from the car. She places a white canvas on the easel tray. Next to the easel, a wooden box holding brushes and tubes of paint, a tin of water and a can of thinner. Her mind is crisp. To the exclusion of anywhere and anytime else, fully in the canyon's grasp, she feels completely at ease, a state of well-being. Her excitement at preparing to paint the canyon, her quickened heartbeat, is no less than when she's about to paint *Pedernal, My Front Yard* from Ghost Ranch.

She notes the folding and unfolding cliffs on each side of her canyon. Bare ridges of cliffs extending into the center of the valley. She notes the fallen rock of avalanches in the canyon and on the valley floor. Patches and stands of trees and bushes precipitously hanging onto cliffs, making their way from the orifice of the canyon out to the valley. She notes how clouds block the otherwise intense sunlight, capturing the range of tropical greens so they can't escape from their habitats in the trees and shrubs, absorbing color as if holding their breath. She notes that she doesn't miss the familiar scarlets and yellows of maples, russets of red oak, and oranges tinged with vermilion of cottonwoods along the rivers. She notes the breeze transporting scents of the ocean.

She notes how form plays with space; how earth plays with sky. How rock plays with plants. How physical, historical, mythological, genealogical, philosophical, ecological and sexual ways of being play with one another.

The canyon notes her quiet demeanor.

12

Waterfall No. 1

*—I am often amazed at the spoken and written word telling me what
I have painted. I make this effort because no one else can know how
my paintings happen—[73]*

Tuesday March 21—Georgia O'Keeffe confesses she's insufficiently versed in 'Īao Valley's divine sensual play of earth and sky. Unlike the outlandishly successful tactics she uses to get people to do her bidding, here, she can't impulsively make the landscape give her what she wishes. She may want to paint, but the clouds and canyon are indisposed to unripe and premature requests. She's unable to vision 'Īao Valley through the same spectacles as she'd visioned Texas, or New Mexico, or Lake Placid, New York. Trusty brushes are useless here. Familiar techniques to paint otherwise familiar landscapes are invalid here. Reds, yellows and purples of the surreal Purple Hills near Abiquiú have no status here. 'Īao Valley abides by its own unique rules, unlike those by which the red sand hills and dark mesas of the Rio Grande abide. Or the blue-greens of sages.[74]

Her mind must be reconfigured. Clouds and canyon will take the time they prescribe to initiate her into their concatenations. Without proper initiation, she'll be frustrated by her attempts to paint the landscape presented to her right here and now. She'll be unable to distinguish rough rock outcrops, discern distances and geometric proportions of chasm walls, and define the heights that waterfalls plunge from pool to pool. She has much to learn.

Their rites of passage will bind her with the operations of nature peculiar to Mauna Kahālāwai's 'Īao Valley. As they deem suitable, they'll begin by unfocusing her perceptions. They'll employ the intense tropical rains common this time of the year that average one inch, easily a half inch, each day to cloud her vision. They'll invite mist and rain, sprinkles and showers, sheets and torrents. They'll confuse her senses and inhibit her otherwise keen ability to discern. They'll make her question everything she sees. They'll simply mess with her mind.

Accordingly, hundreds or thousands of miles away, as if beckoned by the operations of nature peculiar to Mauna Kahālāwai's 'Īao Valley, the heat of the sun evaporates its daily ration of ocean water. Water vapor rises and forms big, puffy clouds. Discrete white clouds. Discrete light chiffon clouds. Discrete pink and alabaster clouds. Discrete straight strings of lacy white clouds. Discrete cotton clouds, envelopes of soft fleece. Discrete light gray corkscrew clouds outlined with orange like three-dimension comic book drawings. Discrete puerile clouds of yellows, ochres, oranges, reds, solid whisks of Payne's gray. All these clouds that Georgia O'Keeffe had seen on the *Lurline* during her ocean voyage to Hawai'i. They set off, carried on the prevailing northeast trade winds.

The valley invites these clouds between its massive basalt arms greeting its visitors from the northeast. Making their way into the valley, and farther into the ancient volcanic caldera, the engorged cloud mass requires space to expand. It needs relief from the tapering confinement. Getting crowded in there, clouds settle onto the valley floor, mount the valley's high ridges and roll down the opposite sides. The cooling valley temperature induces the clouds' metamorphosis, transformed from vapor to rain. The wet massage of the valley a jubilant display of relief.

The natural erotic engagement of clouds and canyon.

The (once-liquid-once-gas-now-liquid) rain exacts the slow, inexorable task of gnawing and sawing into the earth. Like an amiable community of social organisms, droplets of rain fall together onto the ground. Productivity more effective as a collective rather than as individuals, neither hierarchy nor class status distinguishes one droplet from the other. The collective of droplets seeks the deepest cracks, joints and fractures in the rock. The collective also seeks the closest and lowest depressions on the surface of the ground. There the collective gathers as a puddle of water. The collective overflows because the volcanic soil hasn't the capacity to absorb such excess amounts of rainfall in such a short period of time. Gravity forces the collective downhill, and as it flows, it slices shallow swales, rills and gullies into the earth, in which adolescent brooks expand and deepen their potence within the rock and soil. Simultaneously, as is their nature, the adolescent brooks claw back uphill, creating pathways both up and down through which subsequent raindrop collectives will travel, further deepening and clawing.

As all that raindrop artwork inexplicably takes place somewhere up there within the mantle of the clouds, Georgia O'Keeffe imaginatively traces the paths of raindrops on the hidden surfaces creating hidden rivulets, imagines raindrops in hidden rivulets flowing into hidden gullies, imagines water in hidden gullies spilling into hidden ravines, imagines water in hidden ravines streaming into hidden gorges, imagines water in hidden gorges falling into the canyon. Because the canyon is completely embraced by the clouds, she can barely discern the waterfall hundreds of feet above. Were there no rain this day, there'd be no waterfall.

With this scenario, part of Georgia O'Keeffe's rite of passage employed by clouds and canyon, it's seen that she revels in this sensual pluvial engagement rather than disappointedly wishes clouds to dissolve and rain to cease so she can paint. As her response is considered favorable, the clouds gradually evacuate, dramatically revealing the canyon's physical form, shape and structure. Offered this clear vantage, Georgia O'Keeffe envisions how best to begin painting the canyon's natural process of arising, abiding and dissolving.

She hears Arthur Wesley Dow, her Columbia University art teacher, suggest she think about filling space in a beautiful way:

> *Approach art through composition rather than through imitative drawing. Composition is a building up of harmony, the fundamental process in all the fine arts; and harmony is built with three structural elements: Line, Notan, and Color.*[75]

As Dow also had advised, Georgia O'Keeffe begins with a line.

Standing at elevation 680 feet, she retrieves her 7¼ by 4¼ Windsor & Newton sketchbook. Sketching is her meditation, the mental exercise that helps her become intimately familiar with *who she is* and her intimate relationship with the canyon—*where she is*—helping her better understand, assimilate and illuminate the task before her. A sketch helps make the unknown known.[76]

She calculates, in her own mysterious way, without benefit of a topographic map, the geometric relationship between the mountain mass and the canyon it delineates, the relationship between form and space, the relationship between cloud and canyon. Spanning distances from fingertip to wrist, she measures lengths of the two waterfalls as they plunge from one shelf to the next in the midsection of the canyon. She calculates the base of the waterfall 984 feet away at elevation 817 feet; the top of the waterfall 2,165 feet away at elevation 1,282 feet; the top of the ridge .81 miles away at elevation 2,762 feet.

Taking advantage of the lull in the rain—paying no attention that she's skipping two pages of the thin, cream-colored, very smooth woven paper, its "Hareclaw Bond made in England" watermark—she draws two sets of two lines, the upper pair offset to the left. Nine additional lines delineate the outline of the canyon. Eleven pencil lines in total provide a rough outline of the cleaved opening, the crevasse, the V-shape of the valley and the waterfall, a shorthand directive for her brush. An economy of line—yet implicit in its simplicity is the provocative magnitude of elemental forces of rock, water and sky continually carving this landscape. Looks good.[77]

Georgia O'Keeffe begins *Waterfall No. 1* with two lines to define the outer edges of the waterfall. Thinking of *Waterfall No. 1* as a descriptive exploration of the landscape's physical structure, she explores the visible external landscape: the assemblage of topography, geology, hydrology, soils, flora and fauna. She composes with hue, tone and shading. She paints form rather than space. Although she suggests unseen dimensions, *Waterfall No. 1* doesn't reveal the innermost parts of her subconscious intimacy with place. She doesn't touch subtleties of spirit, space, wind and movement. Contains none of the invisible depth recognized by spiritual elders of Maui, intimately connected to their landscape, in which ʻĪao Valley is a personal and indivisible part of their own bodies and hearts, as New Mexico is to hers.

She paints a slit of water plunging over the lip of the rock crest to the left of center of the canyon, dark grayish hue and edges tending to white. She paints the crest as it once projected over the canyon until massive volumes of water, for the duration of who knows how many millennia, shears the edge off, leaving a bare triangle scarp in the face of the cliff and blocks of rockfall covered by tenuous trees and shrubs on the canyon floor below. She paints massive volumes of water, for the duration of who knows how many millennia, notching more deeply into the crest, forcing it to retreat, carving the re-entrant angle in the center of the lip.

She paints the cascading water disappear behind the fallen rockfall, but she doesn't paint the single semicircular rainbow enunciating the water's plunge; it distracts from the entire composition. She paints the water's reappearance below the rockfall debris, diving off another ledge to the right, then a series of pools and falls. No people in the canyon, nor buildings either, even though there's a house at the base, which she doesn't paint either.

Nor does she paint the hidden rivulets, hidden gullies, hidden ravines and hidden gorges feeding the higher waterfall. She appoints a deep dark green to designate that unknown somewhere there. High on the right, a creek behind the sharp, soaring upper mountain ridge is a thin streak of light.

The east and west cliff slopes of the V-shaped canyon are not identical. The east cliffs on the right—their 65-degree slopes—are not quite vertical because the vesicular structure of this oceanic shield basalt doesn't cool with vertical joints. It doesn't produce those sharp, severely hexagonal towers like the Devils Postpile of continental basalt or the Palisades along the lower Hudson River.

Eroded more than the canyon's east side, the 45-degree slopes of the west cliffs reach with less resolve, directly exposed to the million years of atmospheric, ecological and tectonic actions and reactions: tropical winds and rains carried by the prevailing northeast trade winds, tree roots that spasmodically decompose and pry the cliffs apart, cleaving mountainsides, heaving landslides, the detritus of rockfall on the valley floor (geologists call it mass wasting). Almost halfway down, bare basalt rock, as if quarried by a glove, and just below, the expansive talus of rockfall that extends laterally down the mountain slope and spreads across the center of the canyon into the gully, blocking the flow from the upper waterfall.

Intermediate ravines, gullies and gorges of unknown depths, hidden from view, break the west cliff's apparent solidity. Atop, a razor-sharp ridge writhes like a serpent's tail.

Regardless of their physical appearances, so taken is Georgia O'Keeffe by the fantasy of free-flying cliffs to accent the waterfall, she paints the east cliffs on the right almost vertically, and the west cliffs on the left with 70-degree slopes to enunciate the verticality of the right. She paints the hummocky talus hanging on the left cliffs as a broad terrace sloped almost 45 degrees, tree and shrub roots grabbing the ground.

She paints razor-sharp ridges. She paints complex, irregular surfaces of tree- and shrub-covered cliffs as a host of graded shades of green. She paints the interior of the canyon as dark shades of green, exterior slopes as light yellow-greens. She paints deep grays and gray-greens clashing with subtle light tones to boldly delineate edges of dark, plunging ravines into which only plants, birds and clouds would retreat. She paints the

Figure 2. Georgia O'Keeffe, Waterfall, No. 1, 'Īao Valley, Maui, 1939.

puffy cumulus craniums settling into and obscuring the high plateaus between mountaintop ridges and covering whatever remains of blue sky.

Georgia O'Keeffe paints *Waterfall No. 1* to make sense of what she sees. Audacious and brazen, *Waterfall No. 1* is not inclined to mediation with sensitive flower shapes, sinuously soft lines, scarcely perceptible twists nor soft breaths of air. Thoughts and actions bound with one bold stroke directly affect the behavior of all other strokes. Each stroke is a moment, each moment charged with meaning. Nothing is accidental; nothing is incidental. Everything matters.

Her brush capturing the physical appearance of the place, it is most in accord with the moniker used by art historians: "realistic." Testing the waters, so to speak, yet it is the least "real" to her, conditioned by the restrictions posed by everyday appearances most obvious to the common senses and conscious mind to measurable dimensions of form and space, and time.

The valley invites a diaphanous mist to crawl inside from the northeast, a subtle incremental measure of difficulty in the rite of passage, a light drizzle. Her clothes dampen and drops of mist coat her skin, yet she doesn't feel wet at all. She continues to paint. The bits of moisture don't inhibit her. Most strange is that her straight hair turns frizzy.

The misty drizzle is enriched by rain bearing in from the caldera, the center of Mauna Kahālāwai. Clouds and canyon engage with greater intent. Another incremental measure of difficulty in the rite of passage.

She covers her canvas (as I would conceal my camera inside my Gore-Tex raingear 79 years later to keep it dry). The rain briefly stops. Clouds float above the left and right shoulders of the canyon walls, bleeding details Georgia O'Keefe might otherwise imply, and insert themselves into the middle of the canyon.

The valley invites the sheets of rain attending the low, dark nimbostratus clouds of the weather front all the way from the Aleutians. They glide into the valley floor and join the misty drizzle and the rain bearing in from the caldera. An even deeper incremental measure of difficulty in the rite of passage. The entire canyon, with its cliffs, ridges and peaks, is completely invisible to Georgia O'Keeffe. Can't see a thing. She stands there and just watches. After several minutes, the clouds spread, rain lets up, and she sees enough to accent the Wailuku volcanic outcrops with layers of bronze; muted yellow-greens emphasize the edges.

A stand of trees on the alluvial terrace along the stream below the waterfalls. Reaching toward the waterfalls, they enunciate the base of the canyon. She doesn't include them because their presence on the canvas would be a distraction to the composition.

The enrichment of all that misty drizzle and rain bearing in from the caldera, and the sheets of rain carried by the low, dark nimbostratus clouds, engage in what seems to be a capricious, calamitous conspiracy. Georgia O'Keeffe now soaked, Patricia runs to help put her equipment into the car. Georgia O'Keeffe climbs into the back seat, where she again sets up her easel so she can continue to paint the leftover details in the car, as she would under the hot New Mexico sun.

Clouds and canyon now impenetrable, the rain torrential, hardly anything visible, an even more demanding degree of difficulty in this rite of passage. Georgia O'Keeffe packs up her work, climbs into the driver's seat and quickly closes the door. Rain pounding the roof of the car, she gazes through the windshield up to the solid ceiling of saturated deep-gray clouds, looks all around hoping she'll not have to negotiate another vehicle on this forsaken road, now looks down at that ratty three-on-the-floor gear shift. She wonders how she's to ford the rain-pocked river of a road, decides it's better now or never, turns on the ignition, tenuously executes a six-point U-turn and—barely able to see the rough muddy road through the water-smeared windshield and sheets of rain—ever so cautiously manages to keep the station wagons wheels within the faintly delineated road edges, lumbers into town and finally makes it back to the hotel exhausted. Patricia has remained silent the entire way.

After lunch and a nap, she'll finish *Waterfall No. 1*, adding one little cloud hovering up there, a token wisp within the upper canyon, and mist rising from the high invisible stream before its upper waterfall plunge.

(Seventy-nine years later: *Happy safe trails, mister, as you do the same.*)

13
End of Road

Thursday, March 23—Georgia O'Keeffe returns to the valley after Willis and Patricia take leave for Hāna. Willis has left her the car. She drives as far as the road will take her. She drives past Kepaniwai and her canyon. She crosses the bridge onto narrow talus shelves that lift the road high above the stream. The continuous corrugation of ridges and canyons she'd seen yesterday rise above her on the right. Deep canyons spill into the valley on the other side, as well. Skies are clear, for now.

This segment of the ʻIao Valley Road had been constructed over these talus shelves 33 years ago. Rock pulverized and pounded, gravel cleaned and leveled, covered with infertile coarse and fine aggregates formed the base of the single-lane dirt road.

A row of evenly spaced two-by-eight wood posts support two-by-eight wood guardrails three feet above the road surface, meant to provide a degree of security. However, were she to lose control along much of the road, no shoulder would offer to protect her from catapulting over the edge and falling the hundreds of feet to the river. No piece of land would offer to mediate between life and death. Georgia O'Keeffe laughs at the disingenuity that had thought up such absurd safeguards; security taught in the classroom absurdly more dependable than the deplorable physical strength of the railing. A vehicle easily could slide through the flimsy barrier.

The valley dares Georgia O'Keeffe to stop on one of the shelves to paint, but there's nowhere on this harrowing stretch of road that's wide enough for her to pull over, and she's too afraid that she or the station wagon will be struck by another vehicle.

The dirt road ends at a parking lot a half mile beyond Kepaniwai. It feels more like a vestibule to an entry, a foyer to the edge of the sanctuary that marks the origin of the island. Georgia O'Keeffe climbs from the car and beholds a magnificent, green, free-flying vertical cliff that reaches somewhere up there beyond the breadth of the valley, who knows how far, swallowed by the clouds.

The ridge of the free-flying vertical cliff on the right is called Puʻu Kāne, the "Ridge of Creation"; on the left is the Kapilau Ridge, the "Voice of Creation." In the past, these sentinels to the valley granted access only to those trained and endowed with the deepest respect for landscape: the king, the priests and their attendants, and the favored others to whom the royal family granted access.[78]

An attendant ridge of the Kapilau emerges from the clouds. This ridge is capped by rough, ragged triangular teeth, narrow like a serrated knife. Two waterfalls plunge from V-shaped crevasses carved into the ridge. One waterfall, like a strand of silk thread, leaps precipitously onto a shelf of the cliff, emerges from the shelf and veers to the left before free-falling again, disappearing into a stand of trees below. To the right, toward the center of the valley, a second strand emerges through a crevasse that seems less defined, also leaps onto a lower shelf of the cliff, then to the right before diving into the trees below. Long vertical fractures carved into joints of the basalt cliffs will serve as conduits for other strands of waterfall during heavier rains. Were there no rain, there'd be no water falling. Today, there's been just enough to supply the two waterfalls that now appear. Georgia O'Keeffe happily retrieves her sketchbook, makes sure she uses the first pages she'd skipped and sketches the two waterfalls.[79]

As in the canyon, the genealogy of the cliff tells the story of tectonic, geological and ecological forces. Arising, abiding and dissolving. Atmospheric weathering and tenacious tree roots gradually dissolve and pry layers of basalt magma along natural joints and fractures. Earthquakes of no particular magnitude agitate the mountain, cleave outermost layers of rock that buckle, shearing layers of rock from the cliff face that fall as rock avalanche, toppling to the valley floor as talus near the base of the cliff. Vertical scars and bare, ragged outcrops left exposed on the cliff above are smoothed by continuing wind and rain.

The talus rises above a terrace of alluvium composed of boulders and gravel deposited by 'Īao Stream when it roars through the valley, with no particular periodicity, many tens of feet higher than today. Talus and terrace break down, weathering into soil that provides a place for trees, shrubs and vines and their inhabitants to establish. From the parking lot where Georgia O'Keeffe stands, it appears to be about one-third as high as the cliff. She hears the two strands of waterfall jumping unseen through the trees into 'Īao Stream.

A bulging expletive of basalt outcrop bare of vegetation protrudes from a low ridge in the cliff on the left just above 'Īao Stream, a remnant of the edge of the volcano from which magma would explode and lava would proceed to flow at a 7 to 10 percent slope to the ocean. Georgia O'Keeffe can just about make out a striation between the vertical layers marking the volcanic inside and the sloping layers marking outside.

Beyond the break in the cliff, vague layers of ragged cliffs enclose interior canyons. Only imagination and dream seem to be granted permission to enter this narrow portal. The caldera dissuades less mindful intentions. A vortex of wind spills out. Inside seems like sacred space, an untouchable cloud-embraced center. Cool, fragrant damp settles into her skin.

How is she to delineate this gap, the layers of overlapping mountain spurs just beyond, hidden canyons retreating more deeply within? The first sketch is of only three lines—one line delineates the sloped edge of hill on the right, at the end of the parking lot; one line is the stepped edge of the first mountain spur behind, on the left; in the background, the broken line of mountain ridge.[80]

The second and third sketches are more detailed, of many lines. The second sketch attempts to penetrate the V-shaped valley formed by the meeting of mountain spurs, where she imagines ʻĪao Stream flows around the base of each spur, fed by waterfalls from within canyons. For the third sketch, she draws the sloping mountain spurs on the right of the caldera. Each line suggests an additional spur, an additional layer of canyon beyond. One line per spur, one line layered upon the other. Each line a distinct event she must negotiate, an additional moment to comprehend. While attempting to find her way inside, each line is actually an additional layer that removes her from the illusive, mysterious center, never allowing her to reach it. Unable to discern what's going on in there, it all seems vague and indefinite.[81]

She needs a break from the intensity of the portal. She walks down the road a short distance, perhaps five minutes, to the base of the first canyon on the left (to be considered worthy a photo 25 years hence because of the basalt outcrop's uncanny, 50-feet high resemblance to President John F. Kennedy's profile). The first sketch of two lines: solid right slope and broken-lined canyon ridge background. Skipping yet another page, a second sketch: several lines, slopes of the canyon's two sides with its background ridge.[82]

Returning to the portal just below the bulging expletive of basalt outcrop above ʻĪao Stream—another sketch, two lines this time: the heavier marking the basalt outline, the lighter marking the rising slope. Then two more sketches into the caldera, simple lines of rounded mountain slopes and peaks.[83]

Beyond the end of the road above the trees, Georgia O'Keeffe eyes an erect pinnacle. Proud, formidable, the pinnacle is called Kūkaʻemoku— "ʻĪao Needle." A splendid specter headlining all the signs of one singular sensation thrust 1,300 feet in the air, an ejaculation into the sky from the concealed testicle of magma below the earth. An officially designated phallus by none other than the state's Department of Land and Natural Resources, alas, ʻĪao Needle is an eroded remnant of a winding ridge, a chorus line of basalt.

Half a millennium ago, Maui King Kakaʻe conversed with the winds of the valley at the base of Kūkaʻemoku and was advised to designate the valley as sacred grounds. He'd declare it to become his place of burial; subsequent kings would be buried there as well. No one without royal permission would be allowed to make their way up the trail to the end of the valley except during the months of the new year and the harvest. That was then, before the dirt road replaced the trail and the parking lot was built at the end of the road in 1906.

Figure 3. Naoki Kutsunai, ʻĪao Valley photograph, 1937.

Figure 4. Georgia O'Keeffe, *Waterfall, End of Road*, Ĩao Valley, 1939.

Some say Kūka'emoku means "Of the Dawn;" others say it means "Broken Excreta." Still others say it was fueled to erection by labia of the valley, sensitive nerve strands of the island inflamed to excitement by the continual misty wetness. As much as tourist agencies and visitors imagine lurid tales of erotica and snicker, or become inflamed themselves, an organ, however, the Needle isn't.

If she'd hike across the bridge over the tributary flowing into 'Īao Stream, through the surrounding tropical forest and up to the tableland in front of the Needle, Georgia O'Keeffe would see the shaft was an eroded remnant of the knifelike ridge extending across the breadth of the valley, the edge of the volcano now occupied by the caldera.

Georgia O'Keeffe fancies 'Īao Needle as male consort to the V-shaped gap, to the female crevasses and waterfalls of the magnificent cliff. Flights more than fancy, she thinks of landscape and the operations of nature as the play of male and female hills and valleys; female and male ebbs and swells, affairs and formations. The natural erotic engagement of male and female landscapes.

Like she'd written to Stieglitz from York Beach, Maine:

> *The terrific male power in the overpowering breakers as they*
> *move toward you—slowly—but surely coming—and the*
> *same marvelous loveliness that seems female when they break.*[84]

The natural erotic engagement of male and female landscapes—

Expressive patterns of topography and morphology, as visually distinct shapes and spaces remarkably similar to human sexual organs: caves and crevices conspicuously sculpted like vaginas, shrub-covered valleys like mounds of pubic hair, smoothly sloped mountains rising like prominent breasts, and rock obelisks like erect penises. The hermeneutics of geological porn.

The natural erotic engagement of male and female landscapes—

Complements of form and space, of vertical and horizontal landscapes, of projecting and embracing landscapes, of thrusting and receiving landscapes, of probing and revealing landscapes, of giving and receiving landscapes, of light and dark landscapes, of dry and wet landscapes. Makes sense.

However, Georgia O'Keeffe doesn't dwell on this brazen, thrusting male protuberate. Unclad, this autoerotic erection proffers no mystery, neither intrigues nor excites. There's no arising, abiding and dissolution. There's no anticipating, no subtle beckoning, no awkward accepting, no intensifying, no heightening fire nor unrevealed depth, no unexpected orgasmic release. Regardless of its geological and genealogical significance, Georgia O'Keeffe decides not to paint it. This unadorned cock doesn't probe the more subtle depths of landscape.

She returns to sketch the magnificent cliff with its two waterfalls. Like her *Waterfall No. 1* sketch two days ago, an economy of line. Three prominent peaks, the edge of the ridge, crevasses, the sloped layers of basalt that flowed as magma out of the caldera down to the ocean a million years ago, a token treeless outcrop or two. She sketches neither the bare cliff protruding over ʻĪao Stream nor the tree-covered terrace of avalanche and alluvium. Looks good, too.[85]

Georgia O'Keeffe sets her easel near the edge of the parking lot midway between the entrance and the end. As with *Waterfall No. 1*, she paints a descriptive exploration of the landscape's physical structure. An external exploration. Superficial. Yet, like *Waterfall No. 1*, every hue and line matters. Nothing is accidental, nothing merely incidental. Each stroke a moment, each moment is charged with meaning.

She paints three high, ragged triangular peaks. She paints the two waterfalls appearing from the two V-shaped crevasses. She paints the water falling precipitously through narrow vertical gullies in the cliff's severe, green cleavages—grays to white on the left, greenish where the waterfall disappears into a plunge pool on the right. She paints the trees and shrubs hugging the face of the cliff and the long vertical fractures gouging the cliff with deep green, and she paints bare horizontal rock outcrops in gray-greens and black-greens. In the lower left corner, a suggestion of muted ochre and light green treetops growing on talus. Muted and yellow greens graze bare cliff protruding over ʻĪao Stream on the lower right. Light gray underscores puffy cumulus clouds defining sharp edges of the ridge.

No need to climb into her car and set up her easel today. The clouds and valley don't play with her as they did the day before. No mingling, no mist, no light drizzle, no pouring sheets of rain. Today's mix of blue sky and high cumulus clouds keep their distance from the valley. She sees pretty much everything that she wishes, as much as the clouds and valley permit her to see. Painting *End of Road* from the parking lot at the end of the road, ʻĪAO Stream flows below.

After returning to the hotel, she writes to Stieglitz:

> *When I first came to Maui I wrote you about the beautiful green valley—Well—it is a wonderful valley—I've been painting up it for three days and it is just too beautiful with its sheer green hills and waterfalls—I should say mountains—not hills—a winding road that frightens me—big trucks have to stop and back up to get round the curves but even if I'm scared it is worth it—you drive about ten miles an hour—it is just a narrow shelf on the side of the sheer mountain walls—I've borrowed a station wagon from the Sugar Plantation here—I am at Wailuku, Maui[86]*

14

Caldera

—A visual vortex of wild spiral energy—[87]

Thursday, March 23—Georgia O'Keeffe stares from the parking lot through the V-shaped gap of the majestic cliff into the seemingly untouchable caldera. Pleats of clouds fold behind the ridges on each side of the gap, evidence of past 'Īao Stream floods delineated on the gap walls. A portal into unknown origins, would she dare enter and touch that inner space herself?

She stares into the time when earth wasn't ready to birth the islands that would become Hawai'i, when three miles of ocean depth restrained the potential for island making. However, the deep layers of mantle would succumb to the hot spot, a 10,800-degree Fahrenheit furnace within the interior of the earth forging a system of chambers encompassing an area 200 miles in diameter, more or less, far below the middle of the Pacific Oceanic Plate. They'd call this hot spot "Pele's Home." Continuing heat and pressure through the rigid crust would drill and forge the system of deep vertical vents that would serve as conduits for extremely fluid plumes of magma to ascend onto the ocean floor. Emerging fountains of frothing lava, too great for the ocean to contain, would cool into thin layers of gently sloped, dark, iron-rich basalt.

Thus, 1.963 million years ago, Maui was born below the ocean surface from a mound of more than humble circumstances with the birth of an infant Mauna Kahālāwai, a volcanic shield about two million years before Georgia O'Keeffe stands here on the parking lot, looking beyond the V-shaped gap into the ancient center. The subsurface pressure of the deep ocean waters would prevent any gases from expanding, so the magma would harden as a dense, solid, holeless rock, rivers of pāhoehoe.

Eventually, the layered shield of magma would begin to mound above the ocean surface. Released from the captivity of ocean pressure, microscopic specks of volcanic gases could explode within the more fluid magma, producing hole-pocked and mineral-rich crystalline rocks of all kinds. Layers of hole-pocked rocks would sheathe the lower layers of solid, holeless magma rock.[88]

During periods of time lasting one hundred years to two thousand years, depending upon amounts of heat and pressure developed in Pele's Home, magma would be ejected more than once and gradually grow into a teenaged, fully fledged volcanic island, many times taller than the adult Mauna Kahālāwai on which Georgia O'Keeffe presently stands. The expelled lava would flow from the center of Pele's Home as far as the ocean, but no farther, declaring: *Far enough.*[89]

Georgia O'Keeffe stares into the hundred million years of Gaia's locomotion, as the Pacific Oceanic Plate would migrate from one to five inches each year in a northwesterly direction. Simultaneously, Pele's Home, the magma chamber, would slowly migrate southeast. This displacement between the Pacific Plate and Pele's Home would result in the arising, abiding and dissolving of the continuous underwater landform called the Hawaiian Ridge and Emperor Seamount Chain, its islands rising like pedestals above the water.

The island of Hawai'i would be first to emerge from below the ocean. Maui would be the second. Of Maui's two volcanoes, Mauna Kahālāwai would be the older by a half million years, Haleakalā its younger. The two volcanoes would be among the youngest of its 80 brethren, some as much as 70 million years older, having migrated to the northwest, then even more northerly toward the Aleutian Trench. Pele's Home continues to birth new islands farther to the southeast.

As the Pacific tectonic plate carrying Mauna Kahālāwai would continue to migrate from Pele's Home, the volcano's magma source would deplete, volcanism would cease, and Mauna Kahālāwai would be unable to maintain its teenage libido. Burdened with the excess of mass and weight across the expansive breadth of the vent chamber, the volcanic dome would collapse, making a caldera of itself, a huge amphitheater, two miles across.

Georgia O'Keeffe stares into the rumbling waters whose ancestors once flowed astride the highest cliffs of the volcanic remnant, whose 1.3 million years of fluvial clawing, cleaving, chewing, scouring, scraping, slicing, streaming, sheering, deepening, depositing, transporting, eroding, entrenching, expanding, flooding and falling have penetrated the caldera from outside, while simultaneously cascading from inside carrying boulders, rocks, gravel and sand, transporting them down as far as the Isthmus before reaching the Pacific's sea level of that epoch. Streams doing what streams naturally do.

She stares into the early-spring clouds expanding thickly over each of the ridges inside the caldera. Arching winds fan them through the valley. As the day warms and heat rises, the clouds will absorb the heat and just disappear.[90]

She stares at the approaching couple, who've come to ask what she's painting. Georgia O'Keeffe intensely distastes nosy bystanders. She allows no one to see her work until she's finished. The couple doesn't recognize her as the famous artist. They introduce themselves as Gail and Justine, say they've lived on the island for years. They say they also paint. Georgia O'Keeffe asks if they've ever hiked through the V-shaped gap into the center of the caldera. *Of course*, they reply. *We come regularly to plant and help maintain trails through the valley. We're going now.* An unexpected twilight zone, twist-of-fate opportunity presented by these "intruders." Georgia O'Keeffe asks to join them.[91]

* * *

Heavy rains are common these months, likely any time of the year. No official weather organization or system provides rain and flash flood warnings. (It would be another 55 years before the network of telemetered rain gauges of the Hawai'i Monitoring System would be established.[92]) With rains unpredictable, presence in the caldera during a downpour can be hazardous. The massive volume of rainwater spilling down the surface of steep mountain paths has little sympathy for the careless or unprotected and will easily uproot and carry them down the slopes to the river. Floodwaters wouldn't hesitate to transport specks of people, plants or animals downstream and heave them where they'd rather not be heaved. As such, her guides rely on the wisdom of Indigenous Maui people, Kānaka Maoli, who'd advised the couple there'd be no immediate danger owing to their presence in the caldera this day.

Georgia O'Keeffe follows Gail and Justine across the parking lot. Above them, layers of tree-covered cliffs soar, who knows how high. Sharp, ragged ridges, no longer mere lines on her sketch, seem almost as excited as she. She wonders how she's to slip through the shifting slit of a gap between the uncertain folds of the cliffs, even with her guides. Following a short walk uphill, not steep at all, along a shallow slope, they approach the path that would take them up to the Needle. Instead, they turn toward a secondary path downhill in the opposite direction and climb over a makeshift wooden fence on their right, placed there to restrict people from taking the path farther through the woods, where 'Īao Stream had recently overflowed and washed away a section of the alluvial terrace. They descend the 24 makeshift, stone-edged steps that few would attempt—other than Maui residents here for recreation, respite or ceremony—and shuffle down to the terrace just a few feet above the stream.

They circle a mound of loosely piled stones, push their way through a thicket of prickly shrubs and walk the level bank beside the stream on an uneven gray, sandy path. Canopied with several hundred-year-old trees, one of them is recognized by Kānaka Maoli as the grandmother. The tallest and thickest, she's survived more rains and floods than the others, having capitalized on her competitive ecological advantage over kin and others, she's taken charge over the woodlands of this alluvial terrace.

The terrace, an accumulation of sand and gravel deposited by the stream among the larger boulders, covered by soil composed of desiccated leaves over the past few hundred years, is relatively new in the geological scheme. With its regular infusion of deluge and drizzle, the stream's regimen of water discharge and the velocity at which it travels easily can heave the entirety of a tree to the ground and wash a terrace into the river. Her guides have witnessed one day's passage easily different from the another.

*   *   *

Walking beneath the bulging basalt outcrop protruding from the low ridge above 'Īao Stream, Georgia O'Keeffe realizes she's passing through the gap that delineates "inside" from "outside"—"known" from "unknown." She looks over her left shoulder. The high reaches of the waterfall she'd just finished painting appears through the moss-laden canopy from behind the neck of the cliff. How remarkably thin the ridge; how remarkably thin the edge.

Through that indeterminate moment of time, who knows how long, she wonders about the meaning of such a gap, the nature of "passing through"—what does she call it—this aperture, orifice, passage, portal? A crack in space, a broach into a parallel universe? Surrounded by the ring of mountains defining the ring of the caldera, she senses her presence in a landscape unlike the valley on the other side and the human population farther away.

She'd heard of rumors about passages that could whisk you elsewhere, far away in space and in time. There were rumors about people who knew people who'd been transported somewhere else, into some other time simply by passing through such a portal. Even a nondescript, ordinary-looking doorway.[93]

Although most would say this was simply nonsense, the fact is that most people abide in some other place at some other time past or future for the duration of their everyday lives. The misconception in believing one is present here and now when actually they're play-acting, fantasizing lost opportunities as if they'd unfolded otherwise, fantasizing opportunities not yet come to pass to bear fruit: being elsewhere, being another time—rather than living in the present time in the present setting. The ontological oxymoron of "being-there."[94]

She'd heard of rumors about people who knew people who had been released from common everyday appearances and ways of exchange. There were rumors about passages that could whisk you from the profane, jaded domains of everyday existence to the pure lands, sacred realms and nether regions of awakening. There were rumors about the transcendence of body, mind and spirit, if not imagination.

Like the rumors she'd hear about the immutable rabbit hole under the hedge near the bank of a stream that drops straight down into a tunnel as if to the center of the earth or maybe through the earth to the other side, and when landing, Alice would follow the rabbit around corner after corner through a passage to Wonderland.[95]

Like the rumors she would hear about the thin Himalayan crevasse through which Ronald Colman discovers the mystical Shangri-la in *Lost Horizon*, the movie she'd seen two years ago. Like the tornado through which Dorothy Gale discovers the yellow brick road to the magical land in *The Wizard of Oz*, which she'll see after returning to the mainland.

Like the rumors she would hear about the doorway in the back of the wardrobe through which the four Pevensie children discover Narnia in C. S. Lewis' *The Lion, The Witch and the Wardrobe* 11 years hence.

(Like the rumors she would hear about soundless swarm of invisible prickles orbiting clockwise about a foot above the author's head as he bicycles on the narrow secondary road in the mountains north of Kyoto to a temple that hadn't been designated on any map. Its name—*Kim Piera Dai Gong Gen*—is Japanese for "Sublime Place Where Buddhas Appear."[96] And as the ring-like prickling swarm descends, circling his neck, his shoulders, his waist and still-bicycling legs, it never alights. And then as it dissolves, he will have passed into another world 55 years hence).

Georgia O'Keeffe can't put words to it. It feels different here. She'd always thought she had difficulty putting words to what she saw and how she felt. Even if she could verbalize accurately, she'd have to paint to create the equivalent language for anyone else to have a vague notion of her feelings.[97] But here she's at a loss for which neither word nor image can express.

Yet if this is what they call a passage from the profane to the sacred, the transition certainly doesn't appear to have been transcendent. She's convinced she's not ascended into a higher level of consciousness. She tends not to segregate actions and thoughts of everyday life that varied religious dogmas apply to the so-called profane world from invocations to seek higher states of consciousness, numinous transcendence, ethereal emanations and experiences of the so-called sacred. The idea of abiding in a higher state merely seems a designation given to a larger ego, bloated with a sense of self-importance and accomplishment.

She's not passed into transcendence. It's not a train of thought with which she believes or takes comfort; the idea anathema to her anima, a divorce from divinity, a stain on her soul, an incision into her intimacy with landscape that animates and energizes who she is and what she does. The idea of transcendence negates the spiritual richness and beauty of the world in which she lives—her home. Implies a denial of her immediate presence from the landscape of the caldera that so embraces her, and the intimate engagement between them. Neither heaven nor pure land is outside her actuality. This world, just as it is, is that pure land of which they speak. This makes sense to her.

Fully in this world, these soaring ridges, green cliffs, rushing waters, flowers and creatures are as much an expression of divinity or spirituality as the unabashed frocks and implements worn by those who call themselves exemplars of their gods.

Rather, Georgia O'Keeffe is engaged in a rite of passage into a place of refuge: cultivating her grounding in interior quiescence, cultivating her synchronicity with the operations of nature, cultivating in a favorable arena the opportunity to clear obstacles and delusions.

She hears Porphyrus:

> *A threshold is a sacred thing.*[98]

And then she hears from the trail ahead:

Madam, we have to go!

Dead leaves underfoot, kicking aside twisted branches on low shrubs, an occasional large stone indecently tossed by the stream that could twist an ankle, a thin rivulet crossing the path. The three continue making their way. Momentarily sunny, mugginess is blown onto the haunches of the wind emerging from the interior, swirling, taking it out to sea.

*   *   *

They turn from the trail and descend into a gully about as deep as they are tall. Carefully stepping over shallow strands of stream, across a bridge of cobbles and pebbles, just their soles get wet. On other days, when cobbles and pebbles would have been transported and dropped by the stream elsewhere less convenient, their lower legs would be soaked by the crossing.

They climb the opposite bank of the gully. The trail ends a few feet beyond. As they turn right onto a small rise, prickly shrubs and umbrella plants with leaves as broad as their bodies draw blood from their bare arms. Descending from the thicket and turning left, they find themselves on the open terrace bank, exposed to the rambunctious thrashing stream that would drown their shadows where they stand, had the cobbles and large stones not moderated the flow along the bank, and the terrace bank not diverted the stream away toward the gap.

A narrow rivulet separates them from the base of the mountain slope on their right, the base of the first mountain inside the caldera she'd sketched earlier. The rivulet feeds the gully they'd just crossed. With the stream flowing on the left and the rivulet on the right, they stand on a small ephemeral island of cobbles and gravel; ephemeral, for where they stand this late morning is not configured as it was earlier, nor as it will be configured in the afternoon.

Georgia O'Keeffe is struck by the seditious symphony of the descending stream, a choreography of cathartic climatic and geologic events: rushing and rolling, swerving over mounds of stones, black stones and boulders of all shapes and sizes transported and dropped, sweeping over stones and boulders bleached to gray, six inches to two feet across, turned round by the lathe of rushing waters; larger gray-colored boulders kicking smaller stones out of the way and between them gravels of mostly white, gray and black pebbles and gravel with a few of deep reds of varied shapes and sizes covering the streambed. The stream drowns the air with white spray like the foaming froth on the tongue of a wave, pounds boulders as if they were *pahu heiau* ritual drums, *pa ipu* double calabash drums and *pūniu* coconut shell knee drums; or perhaps she hears the pounding of more familiar snare drums and tom-toms, kettles and kick drums, ride cymbals and crash cymbals and splash cymbals were she standing on a small ephemeral island in her own New Mexico landscape and not within the caldera of Mauna Kahālāwai. The thunder of fluvial spates.

No marks or lines in the stream bank delineate a regular periodicity of high and low waters. No transitions mark dry from wet; all is wet underfoot, everything coated in a shiny wetness by the spray of the stream and the 400 inches of rain each year.

A large granitic boulder, pyramid in shape, stained an oily bright, rusty-red iron oxide ahead. Four feet high, five feet width and breadth, this rusty-red triangular boulder must weigh at least 10 tons. Must be the most vibrant, seductive rusty red she's ever seen. Red and pyramid: feminine signs of nature—the state of repose, complement to movement, half the natural order of things.

Another rounded boulder off to the side by the edge of the thicket, bleached-gray, about two feet high and as broad as the red pyramid, its somewhat flat top surface is pocked with small, almost indiscernible holes. In one small depression, standing water of that uncannily vibrant, seductive red, yet nothing of this boulder suggests such a color in its composition or consistency except for the presence of a subcutaneous spirit of its consort, perhaps.

From their backpacks, Gail and Justine each retrieve a pair of small, round granite stones, one red, one light gray, each about an inch in diameter, and a banana leaf. Gail pulls another banana leaf from her backpack, which she hands to Georgia O'Keeffe, along with one red stone and one light gray stone she selects from the ground. Holding her leaf and set of stones aloft, Gail says:

> We bring these from our homes as offerings to the land, waters and sky of Mauna Kahālāwai. Offerings are a reminder that we are conjoined externally, internally and profoundly with the natural process that is the spirit of Mauna Kahālāwai—its hardness and softness, dryness and wetness, heat and cold, inhalation and exhalation—basic components of the cycle of life, a continuing process of cause and effect.
>
> This offering is our token tribute to the mountains for being mountains, boulders for being boulders, water for being water. Our offerings help remind us to revere all grasses, flowers, the forests, the fauna and all of the earth

and the sky. To revere the sun's rising in the east and setting in the west. To revere whatever of nature seems ordinary, to revere what St. Francis of Assisi wrote in the "Canticle of Brother Sun"—

"All praise be yours, my Lord, through all that you have made,
And first my lord Brother Sun,
Who brings the day; and the light you give to us through him."[99]

It makes sense to us that the Lord of which St. Francis writes is the natural process that sees the rising and setting of the sun, the geological formations of Mauna Kahālāwai, the creation and dissolution of this boulder, the storms and droughts that cause the stream to flood and cease flowing is sacred in and of itself, not necessarily the work of a transcendent "other." At its core this is spirituality, and it makes everything right.

We offer the light gray stones to the winds and clouds of the caldera and request protection from the mountain overburden that they easily erode and have descend upon us from above. This mountain movement is the activity of male. We offer the red stones to the waters of ʻĪao Stream and from underground request protection from being deluged. This water movement is the activity of female.

We also make offerings as a reminder to take care while we are here; our presence in the caldera can be tenuous, at best, dangerous at any time, and cannot be taken for granted. With these offerings and thought, we humbly request permission to enter, do our work and leave safely.

They now show Georgia O'Keeffe how to wrap two stones inside a banana leaf, one red stone and one light gray stone within. They each place the two stones inside a loosely rolled umbrella leaf on the level surface of the boulder and silently stand back.

Just above the rivulet on the right, a large gray, rounded boulder lies exposed on the gravel. A horizontal joint, partially covered with light brown and green moss, cements its upper and lower segments. Light green and black lichen spot the boulder above and below the joint. Just below the joint is an etched figure of a person nine inches tall, a petroglyph of indeterminate age: round head, a single straight line for arms, hands pointing down, angular legs that suggest a person running, two semicircles above. Moss grows to the right of the figure without covering it.

Her guides, ready to take their leave, point to an opening in the forest just to the left of the petroglyph stone, with Justine saying:

> This is the trail into the caldera. Indigenous Hawaiian people use it to mark passage to their ceremonial grounds for vision quests and to communicate with the spirits of Mauna Kahālāwai. They also take the trail across the caldera to villages on the opposite side of the island. The narrow passage through the forest gradually climbs astride the stream. Walk past the first flat stone on the left, then turn right at the second flat stone. The trail is not often used, so the forest is thick and likely difficult to penetrate. Be careful with what you do and how you do it. Listen to the spirits, where they direct you and how. They have their ways, so don't go farther afield than they suggest.

Pointing to a steeper trail beside the petroglyph, Justine says they'll be heading up there. Assured Georgia O'Keeffe can find her way back, they instantly disappear in the growth.

Clouds drop off the cliff's shoulder directly above her to the left, revealing a ridge and a pair of pinnacles similar to ʻĪao Needle. A stand of trees covers the base. The ridge appears to be part of the same formation as ʻĪao Needle's. One pinnacle turgid, its lanky twin rises behind as if preparing to lend support, testosterone fueling the formation. It all looks like she'd sketched this, but she's not quite sure.

*   *   *

Georgia O'Keeffe takes the trail as directed by her guides. She hikes past the first flat stone on the left and the second flat stone on the right. The ground flattens and her shoes cake with sluggish mud. Another indeterminate period of time, perhaps 15 minutes, she's like a ball of twine being unravelled by the thick of vines and undergrowth. Seems Mauna Kahālāwai considers Georgia O'Keeffe's continuing hike into the caldera premature. It's impossible to go farther. She'd not anticipated the need for a machete to hack her way through the forest, exposing her to a deeper shade of engagement for which she'd not be equipped. She'd only expected to paint. Thinks it better not to be stupid. Not here, anyway.

A path leads her down to the stream bed on the left. Just a two-foot jump onto the rocks on the edge of the bank. She stands beside an immense rounded boulder, at least six or seven feet across. Ahead, ʻĪao Stream flows slowly in her direction, then around a bare, exposed peninsula of gravel where small trees have attempted to root after the deluge of November 1933 that drowned the entire bank. Then there was the turbulent 1916 storm, of such ferocity that it caused ʻĪao Stream to tear through lands not known to have flooded since. Couldn't say that either storm had moved the boulder beside which she stands.

A distant ridge defines the rough circle of the caldera perimeter of which Maui's highest mountain is part: Puʻu Kukui, its peak 5,788 feet above the ocean. From the right shoulder of the mountain, ʻĪao Stream emerges as a spring and proceeds to carve the landscape of the caldera and beyond to the Pacific. Poʻohahoahoa, a tributary, emerges from the left shoulder.

The adolescent height of the tree canopy directs her line of sight to the upper reaches of the basalt ridges, their natural hexagonal structure contributing to the pattern of erosion that transforms them into what appears to be a rack of dragon's teeth.

Georgia O'Keeffe can't put words to it. Liberated from everyday confines of observed time, she finds herself exceedingly still. Staring over her shoulder, she sees herself painting the waterfall from the other side of the gap that morning; then, sees herself of the morning on the other side staring at her present self at this moment here inside the caldera staring back to the past. And then, staring ahead into the center of the cloud-filled caldera, she observes the chimera of a future Georgia O'Keeffe beginning to materialize. Daring not to anticipate the possibilities, lest she limit the scope of a future, she allows the image to decorporealize.

Liberated from everyday confines of observed time, her sketches of slopes and spurs no longer appear like static nouns at rest. Rather, watches her lines glide through her sketchbook like active notations of motion, like action verbs that have been released from immobility. Point and line, texture and hue, form and space attenuated with arising, abiding and dissolving, swerving through the natural process of motion and rest. Ordering principles of proportion, scale, axis, symmetry, hierarchy, rhythm, repetition and transformation—a continual series of flowing events. Her landscapes become malleable images of continuing time, past to future. How liberating, the idea of drawing noun-verbs, adding dimensions of time to dimensions of space.

Georgia O'Keeffe can't put words to it. Liberated from everyday confines of observed space, she finds herself exceedingly still. She notes that her skin, which she'd normally used to identify the boundary between Georgia O'Keeffe and Mauna Kahālāwai, seems to dissolve. As if she's merged with the caldera, the body parts of Georgia O'Keeffe as the body parts of the caldera, events and thoughts of her life as the entirety of nature.

Except for the particular causes and conditions that determine their individuality, she feels the arising, abiding and dissolving of *who she is* and *where she is* no differently. The operations of nature—earth, water, fire, wind and space—of her own body and mind as of landscape no differently. The softness and solidity of bone and rock, the wetness and dryness of blood and water, the coolness and heat of her private parts and the hot spot of the Pacific Plate, the inhalation and exhalation of lungs and trees no differently. However, unlike Georgia O'Keeffe, nature performs without the hint of ego.

She notes herself inhaling more deeply, like a gift from the caldera. She notes her exhaling, a gift to the caldera, gladly received. She notes while inhaling, air enters an inner world; while exhaling, air enters an outer world, inner and outer intimately as one, her throat like a swinging door.[100]

Then, as if transcribed by the caldera, she hears syllables of Japanese Shingon Buddhist Kobo Daishi:

Differences exist between mind and matter, but their essential nature remains the same. Matter is no other than mind; mind is no other than matter. Without obstruction, they are interrelated. The subject is the object; the object is the subject. The seeing is the seen, and the seen is the seeing. Nothing differentiates them.[101]

And she hears Ralph Waldo Emerson:

Every natural fact is a symbol of some spiritual fact. Every appearance in nature corresponds to some state of the mind, and that state of the mind can only be described by presenting that natural appearance as its picture.[102]

She blends her rhythms with rhythms of the caldera. She inhales and exhales with the same regularity as the ebb and flow of the caldera. Her heart pumps blood cells through her arteries and veins in synch with gravity's pull of each water droplet onto boulders in the stream. Each wave of her hand up and down, each swish of her leg forward and back, each segment of her body a kinetic conversion of energy as is the caldera's accumulation, abiding and erosion of rock.

She hears Carl Jung:

Our psyche is set up in accord with the structure of the universe, and what happens in the macrocosm happens in the infinitesimal and most subjective reaches of the psyche.[103]

Geology transformed into biology, her ovaries like the springs in the magma from which ʻĪao Stream and Poʻohahoahoa appear, her fallopian tubes like the meandering streambeds, her uterus like the widening caldera, her labia like cliff walls of pinnacles and outcrops, her clitoris as alluvial terraces, her vagina the orifice out from the caldera, where she'd orgasmically explode into the valley.

As without, so within.[104]

The sky now clear, in mere seconds, rain and mist will mount the wind. Here she senses: Inside the uterus of Mauna Kahālāwai, made of magma, she stands still. In the sacred center from which she draws inspiration, wisdom and knowledge, she stands still. In the sacred center from which breath is drawn and blood circulates through veins, she stands still. In the organs of nature, the source of sustenance and regeneration of body, speech and mind, she stands still. In the source of Maui's arising, abiding and dissolving of physical form and space, she stands still. In transactions with land, waters and skies, and from which place is indistinguishable from its people, she stands still. In that singular span of time, who knows how long, she stands still.

Georgia O'Keeffe as caldera; caldera as Georgia O'Keeffe.

*   *   *

Must take leave. Georgia O'Keeffe returns as directed by her guides, past the second flat stone on the left, past the first flat stone on the right, past the petroglyph boulder, the red pyramid boulder and the flat offerings boulder. Just below the trail, people splash in the small pools made in the stream's surrender of rocks. One pool just a few inches deep is unoccupied. She rolls up her pants. Warm water. An unexpected drizzle dampens her clothes; surprisingly, her skin remains dry.

She passes beneath the bulging basalt outcrop protruding from the low ridge above ʻĪao Stream, back through the gap in the magnificent cliff between "inside" and "outside." She walks down the road a short distance, sees afternoon clouds nap in side canyons. She draws out her sketchbook. Two wavy lines delineate the canyon above her to the left; three lines delineate the canyon across the valley. Light settles into the colors. Colors fade into gray rain and misty mountains, the active sea ahead.

15

Waterfall No. 2

One sees new things rapidly everywhere when everything seems new and different. It has to become a part of one's world, a part of what one has to speak with—one paints it slowly.[105]

Friday March 24—Georgia O'Keeffe returns to the terrace meadow at Kepaniwai. It would take a unique magic and mystery of such an extraordinary landscape for her to return to paint it—the limitless Texas Panhandle skies, *more like the ocean than anything else she'd known.* Palo Duro Canyon, *slits in nothingness* a thousand feet deep.[106] The family cottage in Lake Placid.

Having moved to her New Mexico homeland 10 years ago, she'd drive 150 miles from Ghost Ranch to the remote Bisti Badlands, the barren, volcanic, gray-black geological ooze that *looks like a mile of elephants, gray hills all about the same size with almost white sand at their feet,* to create over two dozen drawings and paintings of the *Black Place,* a different abstract gathering with each visit.[107]

At first, she'd paint landscape as if through the lens of a camera, inspired by her photographer friend Paul Strand. The queer shapes he'd seek reminded her of Picasso's drawings.[108] Subsequently, she'd want to see landscape in a different light, from a different perspective, at a different time of day and night, under different climatic conditions. To see landscape present itself differently. As *who she is* would be *where she is*, to see herself differently. Depending on the nature of her conversation with landscape that morning or afternoon, with each painting, she'd crop and compress, distend and distort, extract and synthesize, magnify and fete specific features to emphasize or diminish a different part or the entirety of the scene.

What draws her to this canyon in ʻĪao Valley, her valley, her green valley?[109] Open to esoterica, she questions if her rendezvous with this landscape is preordained or meant to be. Is it spiritual will? Divine decree? A cosmic consciousness manipulating the minute operations of mind and nature to accord with a universal code?

More like a karmic collision of sorts, in which previous causes and conditions will have colluded to bring Georgia O'Keeffe and this canyon together. In which case, the encounter could not have taken place any other time in the same way. Nor would it be likely that they'd meet the same way again. While this rendezvous could be construed as a climax of sorts at this particular moment—certainly it's not a climax to either of their lives—rather, the stimulus or charge for subsequent events. One instant in an ever-changing evolution of events. Would her Episcopalian family ascribe to such beliefs?

How does she make sense of what she saw here the other day? How will she make sense of it today? She'll use her brushes to explore the moods and sensations of the canyon like her hands explore the moods and sensations of her lover. Landscape as animated as Georgia O'Keeffe's brush, her brush as animated as landscape. As landscape moves and rests so will her brush, a pirouette of painter and landscape.

Onto a visibly descriptive external landscape, she will layer *Waterfall #2* with her exploration of stories and spirits of geology, genealogy and history. Although it may appear to accord with the moniker "realistic," it will be more real to her than *Waterfall No. 1*, probing more deeply into intimacies of the subconscious.

She finds the precise spot where she painted the day before and sets her easel a bit to the left. She chooses a canvas slightly larger than those on which she painted *Waterfall No. 1* and *End of Road.* Her senses more acute, she listens like the clouds listen, like the rocks and waters, like the geologic formations that build everything up and the ecologic creatures that wear everything down. Like the trees and shrubs and short grasses and animals and snails inhabiting the surface, and the birds flying overhead and building their nests and dropping droppings on the trees and grasses, and the centipedes and millipedes and snails and microbes churning the soil, and the people who worship here and make things here and live and fight and die here. And becoming more attuned to the valley, she begins to add the not-so-obvious moods and stories that have been told and feelings that have been felt and thoughts that have been imagined with a clarity of light and color previously not available for the more familiar, visually descriptive *Waterfall No. 1* and *End of Road.*

She paints the inseparable identity between landscape and its people, the symbiosis of shared physique and breath, their deep love and appreciation in providing for each other, and care for each other. She paints their creative and genealogical chants:

When time turned, the earth became hot

When time turned, the heavens turned inside out

When time turned, the sun was darkened

Causing the moon to shine

This is the time the Pleiades rose in the night

The slime was the source of the earth

The source of the darkness that made darkness

The source of the night that made night the intense darkness,

the deep darkness

Darkness of the sun, darkness of the night

Nothing but night

The night gave birth

Born was Kumulipo in the night, a male

Born was Pō'ele in the night, a female

Born was the coral polyp,

Born was the coral, it emerged[110]

She paints the fundamental operation of the cosmos: the infinitely pure potential of possibilities producing movement and mobility (in Taoism, called yang). When movement consummates its capacity, there is rest and the state of stillness (in Taoism, called yin). When rest fulfills its limit, movement ensues. She paints the alternating cycle of movement and rest driving the force of life and vitality animating all living and inanimate things (in Taoism, chi)—the moment-by-moment cycle of arising, abiding and dissolving.[111]

She paints the earth's migration around the sun, the more or less 190 million miles each year, and paints the obliquity of the earth's axis fashioning the turn of the seasons. She paints the periods of wet and the periods of dry when the north and south hemispheres set their foreheads to the sun. She paints the spin of the earth, the more or less 25,000 miles each day, the days and the nights, the more or less equal periods of light and dark.

She paints this because its stories are bedded with the rock.
She paints the natural engagement of Earth and Sky:

> And out of that mating of Papahānaumoku [Earth Mother] and Wākea [Sky Father] gave birth to the sacred islands ʻĀina, nurturing them in their growth and recession, and from that mating everything in our cosmos continues to come.[112]

She paints the sinews and cartilage of the earth's arising, abiding and dissolving—the orogeny and subsidence, subduction and volcanism, tectonic convergence and mass wasting, bedding and saturation, sedimentation and sheet flowing, aggradation and degradation, deposition and erosion, glacial depression and isostatic rebound.

She paints the hot spot deep in the crust, the straight vertical vents serving as conduits for fluid fountains of frothing lava plumes to rise to the ocean floor and form thin layers upon layers of dark, iron-rich basalt—the volcanic shield of the infant Mauna Kahālāwai—that ascends four miles above the ocean a half million years before Haleakalā deigned to blink. She paints the colossal collapse and erosion, and the second sequence of magma buildup, cessation and subsequent erosion.

Figure 5. Georgia O'Keeffe, *Waterfall No. 2*, 'Iao Valley, 1939.

She paints the ocean's rising and lowering—as much as 400 feet—that accompany glacial advances and retreats during the Pleistocene, separate Mauna Kahālāwai and Haleakalā into distinct islands and repair them back together at the Isthmus. She paints the elevation of sea level determining the course of ʻĪao Stream, the depth that it dissects and widens the valley, and at which level and where its waters saturate the ocean with volcanic debris.[13]

She paints this because its stories are bedded with the rock.

She paints the ancient rush and retreat of rainwater as it seeks the lowest cracks, the deepest joints and the broadest fissures in the 10 to 20 percent slopes of Mauna Kahālāwai, in turn lowering cracks, deepening joints and broadening fissures. She paints accumulating water, funneled as streams, its load of sediments, pebbles and cobbles sculpting and gnawing, scouring and undercutting layers of rock over which the water will cascade and fall and wash away the debris it has carried and cut. She paints the deluge of ancient rainfall alternating with ancient dearth, canyons teeming with heavy streams alternating with bearing no water at all.

She paints this because its stories are bedded with the rock.

She paints the ancient rhythm of a rejuvenated teenage Mauna Kahālāwai, its molten lava shooting up and pouring out from dikes and fissures, repeatedly filling the valley, repeatedly incised by the ancient rhythm of a rejuvenated ʻĪao Stream reworking canyons and cutting new ravines in accord with the revisioned topography—once again incising, once again undercutting, once again scouring, once again clawing backward before being repelled by molten lava, only to begin incising, undercutting, scouring and clawing again.

She paints the ancient rhythm of a rejuvenated ʻĪao Stream, the first of Mauna Kahālāwai's streams to penetrate its once volcanic cone, now depleted of molten lava, having collapsed under its own weight, now a sunken crater: a caldera. She paints the stream expanding the breadth of the caldera and sculpting canyons in the caldera as it does downstream. She paints ʻĪao Stream's capture of less dominant streams in the caldera. She paints the stream cascading into circular swirls, circumscribing plunge pools, further undercutting the caldera terrain and carrying away fallen blocks of magma and eroded boulders.

She paints the confluence of an ancient ʻĪao Stream with waters falling through ancient canyons of the valley, the deposition of boulders, cobbles, gravel and sand forming alluvial fans at canyon bases.

She paints an ancient ʻĪao Stream depositing high deltas of boulders, gravels and pebbles, and the sand dunes along once-upon-a-time shores, winds settling all into place.

She paints the confluence of an ancient ʻĪao Stream with ancient tides, swells and waves of an ancient Pacific Ocean—their rotation its natural practice then as now—when they surged, churned and foamed hundreds of feet higher at the mouth of an ancient valley, when Mauna Kahālāwai was a distinct island. And she paints the confluence of an ancient ʻĪao Stream with ancient tides, swells and waves of an ancient Pacific Ocean—their rotation its natural practice then as now—when they surged, churned and foamed hundreds of feet lower at the mouth of a now remnant submerged ancient valley, when Mauna Kahālāwai was connected to a more expansive Hawaiian landmass.

And she paints the confluence of ʻĪao Stream with the Pacific Ocean, its tides, swells and waves surging, churning and foaming—their rotation its natural practice—at its present level at Paukūkalo Beach.

Painting her love affair with landscape. She paints this because its stories are bedded with the rock.

She paints the bloody encounter that took place the same year Haleakalā last erupted, 1790, the battle of warriors supporting Maui's Prince Kalanikūpule, while his father, Chief Kahekili, sought to unite the islands under his command, against warriors of the Hawaiian leader, Kamehameha, both leaders seeking the same. She paints the great fleet of Kamehameha's canoes that stretched along the entire coast from Kahului to Waiheʻe, and their destruction of Maui's entire fleet. She paints the Battle of the Sand Hills that was fought on the high-level dunes of Wailuku, where the ocean marked its former presence. She paints the battle that moved farther into the valley, where they called the stream Wailuku Stream because so many warriors were killed there, death saturating the water with its blood. Wailuku means "Water of Destruction."

She paints this because its stories are bedded with the rock.

She paints the hand-to-hand conflict on the alluvial terrace at Kepaniwai, the noxious spirit of dead warriors congealed in the soil and on its rocks. She paints the warriors who clawed their way up the canyon's rock precipices and outcrops, attempting to escape Kamehameha's pursuit. She paints the warriors who fell hundreds of feet to their deaths in the battle called Kaʻuwaʻupali, meaning "Clawed Off the Cliff." She paints the noxious spirit of a battle so fierce, the ground saturated with enough dead bodies to construct a dam and block the flow of ʻĪao Stream beyond. There they called the battle Ke Paniwai o ʻĪao, meaning the "Water Dam of ʻĪao," the battle that united the Hawaiian Islands under the rule of Kamehameha at the expense of Maui Chief Kahekili and his son, Prince Kalanikūpule.[114]

She paints this because its stories are bedded with the rock.

She paints movement and stillness from the beginning of time, the steady-state equilibrium between rock and plants and sky, between acting and quieting, between growing and diminishing, between going and coming, opening and closing, filling and receding, thrusting and retreating, absorbing and regurgitating. She paints the incremental moment-by-moment magic of nature's operating, the rhyme of cause and effect.

She paints lines, colors and textures more vividly than those of the first painting. She paints ridges more defined, outcrops more distinct, water more assertive, the canyon's V shape sharper. She paints no clouds taking shape within the canyon; only sheathing high background mountain peaks.

Painting her love affair with landscape. She paints this because its stories are bedded with the rock.

Feeling ʻĪao Valley is now her valley, as with any intimate relationship, they've much to learn of each other, a gradual revelation of their most accessible and their most intimate parts.

Emerging from the valley   full from the day
the younger Haleakalā rises beyond
its full entirety   elegant simplicity.

16

Waterfall No. III

—The abstraction is often the most definite form for the intangible thing in myself that I can only clarify in paint—[115]

Sunday, March 26—Returning to the terrace meadow at Kepaniwai, Georgia O'Keeffe looks deeply into the canyon's subtleties of spirit, space, wind and movement. Two thoughts come to mind. The first speaks to rhyme: *Waterfall No. III* will be an expression of her emotional state. The second speaks to reason: *Waterfall No. III* will confirm her search of truth.

*   *   *

First, painting is the creative act of her heart, and the operative nature of her heart is to create beauty.[116] As an artist, she penetrates deeply into her feelings, even if she doesn't understand them. She paints thoughts of her heart rather than intellect spilling from her head. Without disavowing anything of her life, intent on harnessing all in its entirety, she imaginatively crafts her intimate engagements with people, places and things: the impetuous dramas, the encounters and affairs. She extracts exciting pleasures and natural propriety, art and landscape as expressions of wonder, joy and anguish, love and hatred, ecstasy and terror, her truths and her lies—libido's excitation. She paints color and texture rather than phrase and paragraph, joy and anguish rather than analysis and conjecture, the texture of rhyme rather than the oracle of reason.

Unlike her friends and critics, their sexually absorbed commentaries more likely in dialogue with their private body parts, her widely acknowledged expression of sex is not the source of her inspiration. Her paintings' idiosyncrasies express feelings she's had that are unlike others'. She'd long ago concluded:

> *Even if I could put down accurately the thing that I saw and enjoyed, it would not give the observer the kind of feeling it gave me. I had to create an equivalent for what I felt about what I was looking at—not copy it.*[117]

*   *   *

Second, she's an artist in search of truth. Not disavowing anything of her life, she'll harness its entirety. *Waterfall No. III* will be an inquisition into the depths of who she is and who she wants to be. She'll give order and meaning to what is most real to her, excite her sense of pleasure and natural propriety. She'll plumb the depths of all that the canyon and she can know of each other, not limited to apparent appearance. Through each stroke of paint, she'll explore those subtleties of spirit, space, wind and movement inside and outside, whatever and wherever the delineations between them.

She hears Muso Soseki, 14th-century abbot and designer of Kyoto temple gardens Saiho-ji and Tenryu-ji:

> *There are people for whom landscape sustains their search for truth—this is truly noble, for there is no distinction between love of landscape and a search for truth. These people will see the great earth of mountains, rivers, trees and stones in their changing appearances through the four seasons— as a means to search for truth in their making (and painting) landscape.*[118]

Previous works now seem quaint, served by familiar techniques and brushwork from the cache of tools and experience brought from the continent. ʻĪao *Waterfall No. 1* and *End of Road* provided the means to understand the physical characteristics of the canyon. Although "realistic" in appearance, they were the least real to her. The least truthful. ʻĪao *Waterfall No. 2* helped illuminate genealogical and geological stories. While penetrating depths not necessarily visible, while "realistic'" in appearance, ʻĪao *Waterfall No. 2*, also was not as real. Not as true.

As *Waterfall No. III* evolves, infused with feelings of her inner "abstraction" of landscape, the image revealed by the formation of clouds and canyon will appear more real and true to her than the previous three paintings. More real and true to her than the descriptive ʻĪao *Waterfall No. 1*. More real and true than the spirit of stories, metaphor and myth of ʻĪao *Waterfall No. 2*. It will possess more substance, more truthfulness to what she feels. All she knows is that it's what she needs to do.[119]

Looking deeply into subtleties of spirit, space, wind and movement, she's nourished by memories. They spark inspiration. She recalls the 58 Brancusi pieces she'd studied at the Brummer Gallery in 1933. She'd read the *New York Times* headline: *Brancusi Exhibition at Brummer Gallery Hard on Realists but Highly Pleasing to the Imaginative*. In the exhibition catalog, Brancusi had written:

> *Do not look for obscure formulas or mystery. It's pure joy that I give you. Look at these sculptures until you see them—as those who are closest to God have seen.*[120]

She recalls Brancusi's 1922 oak sculpture of *Socrates*. It looked nothing like a body should look. And she thinks about what Brancusi had said of Socrates:

> *Nothing escapes the great thinker. Eyes in his ears, ears in his eyes; he knows all, sees all, hears all.* Then she thinks about what Brancusi had said about her own work: *There is no imitation of Europe here; it is a force—a liberating free force.*[121]

Looking deeply into the canyon, she doesn't know what she'll paint, from where this image will come, nor how. Programmed intentions to probe particular fashions would obviate the effervescence of the creative, candid process. Anticipation and expectation would merely lead her to wish for fulfillment exacting conditions and qualities of lesser import. Immediacy and intimacy abide in her independence from limits posed by wishes, desires and thinking. Alas, she must pocket them.

She'll approach the next painting differently. Her search for truth commands a plunge into places she's not gone before, to paint *Waterfall No. III* through media she's not traveled, to feel what she's not touched. Creativity in the search of truth will depend upon her openness to the full plunge into the caldron, the full catastrophe, even if she has no parachute, so to speak. No problem; there's no ground onto which she'll fall.

As seemingly simple as Isaac Newton's three laws of motion, and the mystical complexity of Buddhist laws of interdependence, the subtle motions of clouds and canyon will guide the flowering of Georgia O'Keeffe, as Georgia O'Keeffe guides the unfolding of clouds and canyon.

Perhaps she'll begin *Waterfall No. III* with straight lines until otherwise convinced or compelled to change by clouds and canyon—their light, heat, gravity, moisture, chemistry—when she'll match with a calculus of curves. The action of each stroke matched by an equal and opposite reaction from clouds and canyon.[122]

Perhaps the clouds and canyon are intent on teaching Georgia O'Keeffe the profound reality of the operations of nature. She recalls Arthur Wesley Dow's Buddhism having mentioned Nagarjuna's *Prajna-paramita*: the totality of relative truth, in dependence upon causes and conditions: arising, abiding and abating within as without, the symphonic rhyme of cause and effect. As such, she'll picture an animated marriage with the clouds and canyon in dependence upon each other's presence and disposition, as the Tibetan Mahayana Buddhists say:

> *It is because of the collective karma of all sentient beings that*
> *the earth is round.*[123]

Questioning the presence of a boundary between her psyche and the psyche of clouds and canyon, she'll still reckon an appearance of an outer world,[124] her physical state arising in dependence of landscape, the events portraying the rhyme and reason of her life originating as much from the exotic and erotic play of clouds and canyon as from her own heart. Perhaps the source and feelings of love and anguish, imagery and language giving expression to *Waterfall No. III* will originate from the psyche of her "outside" landscape rather than her "inside" landscape.

Fueled by what she feels as by what she sees, she'll probe the subconscious intimacy lurking between Georgia O'Keeffe and the clouds and canyon, between mind and landscape, serving a portrait of clouds and canyon as a self-portrait—Georgia O'Keeffe outside her skin and landscape within—questioning who's Georgia O'Keeffe and who's the clouds and canyon. Selecting, deleting and emphasizing things imagined and felt. Nothing unreal nor untrue about that.[125]

If Georgia O'Keeffe feels more at ease, perhaps her temperament is a reflection of the clouds and canyon at ease. Likewise, perhaps the clouds and canyon seeming more at ease is a reflection of Georgia O'Keeffe's ease. Georgia O'Keeffe and the clouds and canyon, mind and landscape, seemingly distinct organisms, actually one. As clouds loosen, engaged in their primal ecological yield to the wind, current and pressure in the air, so do her shoulders drop, unburdened by predilections.

Previous days of clear skies and relaxing clouds provided her with the entire cinemascope of cliffs and waterfalls, the valley and the canyon. Its glorious full frontal enabled her to paint its form, paint its stories. She knows that the clouds and canyon weren't necessarily yielding to Georgia O'Keeffe. Like anything of landscape, like anything of her life, the basic natural law of weather is to change, as if a continual process of dissatisfaction with the present. Buddhists call it the truth of suffering. Clouds and canyon call it the truth of weather, mere engagement in their primal ecological posture. Regardless of their relationship, it wouldn't matter what she'd come to see.

She acknowledges the perversity to the creative process to anticipate or wish for weather to remain as is. She smartly sets aside hopes to be rewarded with amenable climatic conditions allowing her to continue visually penetrate the canyon. Better to relish the present rather than wish for amenities of the past and expectations of amenities continuing in the future. Best she's willingly open to whatever is presented. Loath to preoccupy herself with words, she has no wish to burden the clouds and canyon with an excess of foolish requests.

A bird soars above the talus. Seems huge. She measures its wingspan between the tip to the crease of her thumb. Almost two feet long. Perhaps a white-tailed eagle, *Haliaeetus albicilla*. Rare on the island, seen widely in northern Europe and Asia; but so much that's foreign, both plants and people, have been introduced from elsewhere. More likely it's a Hawaiian hawk, what people call the *'io*. The male soars on the updrafts looking for rodents for lunch, its shrill, high-pitched *EEEH-OH* reverberates within canyon walls. Its sharp eyes on its mate, who sits on the single egg in her nest in the branches. Majestic. She adjusts her easel to sit stably on the ground.

*   *   *

She'd written to Stieglitz 11 years ago from York Beach, Maine, seduced by the illumination of landscape's most private parts, the roll between movement and rest:

> *You say you wonder how the ocean looks to me—This morning I was thinking of that to myself—As terrifically male and female as ever— the same terrific male power in the overpowering breakers as they move toward you—slowly—but surely coming—and the same marvelous loveliness that seems female when they break—*[126]

John Vanderpoel had taught her at the Art Institute of Chicago that painting the angles and curves of landscape was like painting the sharpness of her jaw and the curvature of her thigh. Photographing erotic curves of her body, Stieglitz presented her as landscape.

She questions if she's come to paint *Waterfall No. III* as the erotic play of Dionysius Areopagite's theology—spiritual intellect moving circularly when uniting with illuminations of the "beautiful," female cause and effect of the natural process, and the "good," male pure consciousness, without beginning and end; and moving in a straight line when proceeding into providences they are said to direct.[127]

She questions if she's come to paint *Waterfall No. III* as the erotic play of yoga art—erect male lingam the expression of pure consciousness purusha, the essence of the universe, in union with receptive yoni, the operations of nature and cosmic energy prakriti. Erect male lingam delineated as a triangle pointing upward; receptive yoni delineated as triangle pointing down. The erotic engagement of phallic thrusting and female embracing circumscribed within the circular wheel of arising, abiding and dissolving.[128]

She questions if she's come to paint *Waterfall No. III* as the play of erotic geometry—angles as signature of sexually charged male geometry, curves as signature of sexually charged female geometry, like Edmund Burke's sensuality of male-driven sublime landscape with embracing female landscape of the beautiful.[129] The erotic engagement of phallic thrusting and female embracing.[130]

166

She hears Carl Jung:

How few things there are that can't be reduced to the instinct of sex. Our psyche is set up in accord with the structure of the universe, and what happens in the macrocosm happens in the infinitesimal and most subjective reaches of the psyche. Whether called libido or primordial psyche, the instinct of sex is the driving strength of our own soul. It makes life proceed. It's the love for life, the creative instinct for the beautiful, for the strength to fabricate good and avoid the not so good.[131]

She questions if she's come to paint the inflamed ardor between clouds and canyon as intimate parts of her body so engaged, exploring clouds and canyons as her lover, as she'd written Stieglitz 17 years ago, again from York Beach, Maine:

I am on my back—wanting to be spread wide apart—waiting for you—to die with the sense of you—the pleasure of you—the sensuousness of you touching the sensuousness of me—All my body—all of me is waiting for you to touch the center of me with the center of you—

Dearest—my body is simply crazy with wanting you—If you don't come tomorrow—I don't see how I can wait for you—I wonder if your body wants mine the way mine wants yours—the kisses—the hotness—the wetness—all melting together—the being held so tight that it hurts—the strangle and the struggle—the release that moans and groans and the quickly drawn breath—the reaching of something in the whole body for the center of heaven—[132]

She imagines the slightly bent tips of her deft brush, deliberate strokes, anticipatory delight offering the least resistance. Excited clouds skimming the surface of her skin, saturated juices of rain moistening her belly and her sex, inducing an amorous and not unpleasant enjoyment, heated desire, hotter with the scent of oil, whites and green-grays, prolonging mystery, yielding with pleasure.

She imagines her soft bristles guiding the sinuous weave of the volcanic waterfall. Releasing springs from underground, disengaged from the hollows of the mountain by her fingertips, flowing between folds hidden behind mountain peaks. Aroused by the tickle of low mosses and ferns lining the fine slit cut into the middle of the ledge, waters rapidly plunging over the broad triangular scar, the splash hidden behind trees and shrubs covering the rockfall, the reemerged trajectory orgasmically pouring onto the lower pools between the spreading thighs of canyon walls. Its merging with ʻĪao Stream.

And she thinks: By painting the canyon, I paint my life.[133]

*   *   *

Initiated into the most conscious and conscientious third shade of engagement with landscape, she sharply fixes her senses into the canyon, into subtleties of spirit, space, wind and movement—aspects of the landscape known by those spiritual elders intimately connected to the valley, as personal and indivisible to their hearts and bodies as New Mexico is to Georgia O'Keeffe's. In turn, the canyon notes her quiet demeanor.

Perhaps she's gotten it wrong; perhaps she's not come to paint a "thing." Perhaps she's not come to paint the obvious, to delineate the shape of the canyon, the fall of water, the slope of walls, the weight of form. Perhaps she's not come to capture the canyon and its waterfall as if permanent when laws of impermanence make the actual capture of the canyon unlikely.

Moreover, perhaps she's gotten it wrong: perhaps she's not come to paint space and form of landscape as erotic curves of her body. Perhaps she's not come to paint lines, textures and volumes, contours and angles of landscape as depths of her soul. Not come to paint tone and color of mist and clouds as tears of her laughter and sorrows. Not springs emerging beyond cliffs as the flow of juices from her vagina. Not the liminal line between earth and sky as winds gracing her body. Not sky and earth, clouds and canyon as the private providence of her body parts.[134]

(Seventy-nine years later, nor have I come to sketch a "thing.")

No, painting *Waterfall No. III*, she doesn't succumb to the allegorical anthropomorphizing of clouds and canyon as sexual body parts. As she hadn't succumbed to the continuing saga of lurid chatter and innuendos, critics and friends alike—Herbert Seligmann's description of her "breastlike contours of cloud and the black cleaving of lake shore," Marsden Hartley's "shameless private documents with an unqualified nakedness of statement,"[135] Lewis Mumford's "one long, loud blast of sex."

Painting *Waterfall No. III*, initiating the vortex of swirling, shifting clouds circling canyon walls, she paints the mysterious, irrefutable *GEOPOMORPHIZING* of Georgia O'Keeffe—the natural operation of landscape as her muse. Geopomorphize, derived from the Greek, *geō–*, "earth,"

Figure 6. Georgia O'Keeffe, *Waterfall No. III,* ʻIao Valley, 1939.

and *morphē*, "form": ascribing characteristics of geologic form and space to human characteristics, in contrast to, and casting doubt on, anthropomorphic penchants to ascribe human characteristics to the geologic.[136]

Meeting her maker, as clouds and canyon meet theirs, she paints *who she is* as *where she is*. Paints as landscape might paint Georgia O'Keeffe, under her skin, deep in the heart of her. Paints the geopomorphizing of Georgia O'Keeffe—human form and space as the natural operation of arising, abiding and dissolving of geologic form and space.[137] Muse to landscape, she paints Neruda's

> *I want*
> *to do with you what spring does with the cherry trees.*[138]

Geopomorphized, Georgia O'Keeffe doesn't paint body parts; she paints the natural erotic engagement of complementary pairs—

She paints the alternating cycle of movement, the fundamental flourish of male operations, and rest, the fundamental quiescence of female operations, that together drive the force of life and vitality animating all living and inanimate things (in Taoism, chi)—the moment-by-moment cycle of arising, abiding and dissolving. She paints male and movement as the heavens, the sun, mountains and height, summer and heat and the sunny side, the south, aridity, motion, growth and life. She paints female and rest as the earth, the moon, valleys, ravines, rivers and caves, the dark side, winter and cold, the north, moisture, stillness, decay and death. She paints movement with rest, active with passive, day with night, summer with winter.[139]

Figure 7. Dennis Alan Winters, *Canyon sketch,* 2018.

Geopomorphized, Georgia O'Keeffe doesn't paint body parts; she paints the natural erotic engagement of complementary pairs—

The operations of her body and thoughts of her heart functioning as sensual animation of landscape. The engagement of hardness and softness, dryness and wetness, heat and cold, and breath composing Georgia O'Keeffe as the engagement of hardness and softness, dryness and wetness, heat and cold, and breath composing landscape; the same processes of arising, abiding and dissolving in Georgia O'Keeffe as in landscape. Just as Ernest Fenollosa had written that the structure of Chinese language is based on the operations of nature, so does her sexuality engage as the operations of landscape.[140]

Geopomorphized, Georgia O'Keeffe doesn't paint body parts; she paints the natural erotic engagement of complementary pairs—

The primal presence of landscape fueling Georgia O'Keeffe as the presence of Georgia O'Keeffe fuels landscape—qualities of one in dependence upon qualities of the other—she paints the mating of form and space, the marriage of sky and earth, the embrace of wind and rock.

Geopomorphized, Georgia O'Keeffe doesn't paint body parts; she paints the natural erotic engagement of complementary pairs—

The dialectics of earth, waters and skies—orogeny with subsidence, subduction with volcanism, tectonic convergence with mass wasting, bedding with saturation, sedimentation with sheet flowing, aggradation with degradation, deposition with erosion, glacial depression with isostatic rebound.

Geopomorphized, Georgia O'Keeffe doesn't paint body parts; she paints the natural erotic engagement of complementary pairs—

The dialects of landscape—form and space, inward and out, rise and fall, thrust and receipt, push and pull. She paints vertical landscape fueled with horizontal landscape, convex landscape with concave landscape, dry landscape with wet landscape, hot landscape with cold landscape, lit landscape with darkened landscape, inner landscape with outer landscape, the offering of rain and drizzle with the receipt of outcrops. Spires, ridges and peaks thrust into the cloud's pockets of mist.

Geopomorphized, Georgia O'Keeffe doesn't paint body parts; she paints the natural erotic engagement of complementary pairs—

The breath of V-shaped space with the tangibility of V-sculpted cliffs, landscape that projects with landscape that embraces, landscape that penetrates with landscape that accepts, landscape that probes with landscape that reveals. She paints landscape that supplies with landscape that receives, landscape that invites with landscape that repels, centrifugal landscape that absorbs with centripetal landscape that expands, landscape of the light with landscape of the dark. She paints lava plugging vent, rainbow brushing rock, wind whisking water, root penetrating crevasse, rain vaccinating soil, crickets filling quiescence.

Now disciple of breath of space rather than the weight of form, disciple of cloud rather than cliff, of mist rather than outcrop. She paints clouds riding wind, creeping over ridges and terrace, sliding into folds, penetrating valley and crevasse, filling amphitheater, the magnetic vibration of cloud and cliff, a millimeter of electric breath between. Disciple of clouds, heart of her subject, where otherwise she'd think they were just plainly getting in the way.

Georgia O'Keeffe doesn't paint body parts—

She paints drizzle blotting sky, mist masking cliffs. She paints the vortex of vapor circling deep recesses of the canyon, thick sheets of rain where waterfall should be, swirling winds and lateral currents confining its spread, wet margins seriously coiffed, a "French curve." She paints opaque sheets of thick gray molded like an isosceles triangle, elongated from top to bottom, sheathing the canyon from crest to its midriff talus.

Georgia O'Keeffe doesn't paint body parts—

She paints cloud split into two, slit from top to bottom, folded and massaged into its succulent wet core, the slit's wetness painted as a clear white line. The cloud swelling with condensed evaporate on each side; thickening, its outer edges folding back into dark gray, the entirety perforated with wetness. The waterfall released below, the natural erotic engagement of complementary pairs, falling and pooling, falling and pooling.

Georgia O'Keeffe doesn't paint body parts—

She paints landscape and Georgia O'Keeffe, consensual partners engaged as nature's animation. She paints her truths and her lies; her wonders, joy and anguish; her loves and suffering; her ecstasies and terrors.

Appearing to accord with the moniker "abstract," she doesn't paint an apparition. To Georgia O'Keeffe, *Waterfall No. III* is the least restrictive, the least insecure, the least conditioned and least expected. Hence, the most embracing, the most reflective, most definite form for the intangible things in herself that she can clarify only in paint, the most accurate image appearing to her heart, visually apparent to the deepest, most expansive parts of her psyche. A truth as real and substantial as anything she'd realized in her life. A self-portrait.[141]

She paints *Waterfall No. III* as she'd not painted before. Back when teaching in Texas, she'd torn all her work, thinking them mere copies of what others had painted, not her truth. She still wants to be the one who discovers, not the second or third. Better to be ignored than a has-been.[142]

The York Beach pleasures recede behind this natural erotic play of clouds and canyon. She paints her coming-to-be rather than her having-been. She paints the most real, the most "Georgia O'Keeffe." She paints Rilke's

> *Earth, isn't this what you want? To arise in us, invisible?*
> *Is it not your dream, to enter us wholly*
> *there's nothing left outside us to see?*[143]

A rainbow breaks from the arms of the valley
amplifies above the Isthmus haze
the distant view framed   &   embraced
outside form   &   space   drawn in
blending the not visibly apparent with imminence
landscape captured alive.
Absorbed by the pure   luminescent cerulean blue of the sky
she feels   *who she is*   indistinct from   *where she is.*
Winds blowing from the northwest   anticipate a storm front.
Haleakalā   beyond
drifting off in space someplace.[144]
Georgia O'Keeffe—*far away in another world here.*[145]

17
Tuesday, March 28

Wailuku: *In about three hours I am leaving Maui for Hawaii. I am sorry to go—I like it here—It is easy to get around as things that are very good are near by. I have five paintings—from Wailuku—two from Hana—A very good island—much more like an island than Oahu—*

A kiss to you as I am leaving it I go by boat over night—will be there early in the morning. . . .[146]

18

Exhibition of Oils and Pastels
February 3 – March 17, 1940
An American Place
New York City

If my painting is what I have to give back to the world for what the world gives to me, I may say that these paintings are what I have to give at present for what three months in Hawai'i gave to me.

Some of them were painted in Hawai'i, some were painted here in New York from drawings or memories or things brought home.

What I have been able to put into form seems infinitesimal compared with the variety of experience.

One sees new things rapidly everywhere when everything seems new and different. It has to become a part of one's world, a part of what one has to speak with—one paints it slowly. One is busy with seeing and doing new things—one wants to do everything. To formulate the new experience into something one has to say takes time.

Maybe the new place enlarges one's world a little. Maybe one takes one's own world along and cannot see anything else.[147]

—Georgia O'Keeffe

GRATITUDE

Thank you   Elissa Gallander   even so

Thank you   Arnie Kotler   for your continuing advice & support
introducing me to Patricia & other things of Maui   &   as my agent
for helping to guide this to fruition

Thank you   Lauren Schiffman of Editcetera for your meticulous
& diligent copy-editing   your attention to words   &   spaces   &
helping to make the story flow

Thank you   Richard Kutsunai   for your stories of the Valley &
gifting me the 1937 photographs taken by your father with your
permission to reproduce them with my writings

Thank you   Memphis Brooks Museum of Art   Honolulu Museum of Art
& Georgia O'Keeffe Museum   for permission to reprint the paintings

Thank you   Tori Duggan   Georgia O'Keeffe Museum
Research Collections & Services Associate   for your valued assistance

Thank you   *Kanaka Maoli* of the Maui Historical Society for sharing
some of the magic

Thank you   David Palmer   for your friendship & support for reading
early iterations of the manuscript

Thank you   Lars Bermann   for years of friendship & support

Thank you   Linda Berry   for introducing me to the Valley   & other things of Maui

Thank you   Suzanne Bott   for introducing me to the waterfalls

Thank you   Architecture, Culture & Spirituality Forum   for the opportunity to present the book capsule at Taliesin West

Thank you   Connor Wolfe   publisher of Outpost Press for making this happen

Thank you   Earth   Waters   &   Sky

Sources

Georgia O'Keeffe: Autobiographical and Biographical

Barson, Tanya. *Georgia O'Keeffe*. London: Tate Publishing, 2016.

Dijkstra, Bram. *Georgia O'Keeffe and the Eros of Place*. Princeton, NJ: Princeton University Press, 1998.

Giboire, Clive, ed. *Lovingly, Georgia: The Complete Correspondence of Georgia O'Keeffe & Anita Pollitzer*. New York: Simon & Shuster Touchstone, 1990.

Greenough, Sarah, ed. *My Faraway One: Selected Letters of Georgia O'Keeffe and Alfred Stieglitz: Vol. 1, 1915–1933*. New Haven, CT: Yale University Press, 2011.

Groarke, Joanna, and Theresa Papanikolas. *Georgia O'Keeffe: Visions of Hawai'i*. New York: New York Botanical Garden, 2018.

Hartley, Marsden. "Georgia O'Keeffe" In *Adventures in the Arts: Informal Chapters on Painters, Vaudeville, and Poets*, 116-119. New York: Boni and Liveright, 1921.

Haskell, Barbara, ed. *Georgia O'Keeffe: Abstraction*. New York: Whitney Museum, 2009.

Hinton, David. *The Wilds of Poetry*. Boulder, CO: Shambala Publications, 2017.

Jennings, Patricia. *Georgia O'Keeffe's Hawai'i*. Kihei, HI: Koa Books, 2011.

Keller, James M. "Pineapple Expressionism: Georgia O'Keeffe and Ansel Adams in Hawaii." *Santa Fe New Mexican,* Feb. 7, 2014. http://www.santafenewmexican.com/pasatiempo/art/museum_shows/pineapple-expressionism-georgia-o-keeffe-and-ansel-adams-in-hawaii/article_a6c9b963-62c8-5b8e-b276-730539c101de.html

Letters from O'Keeffe to Stieglitz. From Alfred Stieglitz/Georgia O'Keeffe Archive. Call Number YCAL MSS85. Beinecke Rare Book & Manuscript Library – Yale University Library. New Haven, CT. https://orbis.library.yale.edu/vwebv/holdingsInfo?bibId=4043529

Lynes, Barbara Buhler. *Georgia O'Keeffe: Catalogue Raisonné.* New Haven, CT: Yale University Press, 1999.

Lynes, Barbara Buhler. *O'Keeffe, Stieglitz, and the Critics, 1916–1929.* Ann Arbor, MI: UMI Research Press, 1989.

Lynes, Barbara Buhler, Ann Paden, and Sarah King, eds. *Maria Chabot— Georgia O'Keeffe: Correspondence 1941 -1949.* Albuquerque, NM: University of New Mexico, 2003.

Lynes, Barbara Buhler and Carolyn Kastner. *Georgia O'Keeffe in New Mexico: A Sense of Place.* Santa Fe: Museum of New Mexico Press, 2012.

Marshall, Richard. *Georgia O'Keeffe: Nature and Abstraction.* Milan: Skira Editore, 2007.

Odall, Sharyn. *O'Keeffe and Texas.* New York: Harry N. Abrams, 1998.

O'Keeffe, Georgia. *Georgia O'Keeffe.* New York: Viking Press, 1976.

Saville, Jennifer, ed. "Off in the Far Away: Georgia O'Keeffe's Letters Home from Hawai'i." *The Hawaiian Journal of History* 46 (2012).

"SS Lurline Forum." Encyclopedia Titanica (comments on website), Nov 25, 2017, June 15-16, 2018. https://www.encyclopedia-titanica.org/community/threads/ss-lurline.24974/page-2#post-398867

Tompkins, Calvin. "Georgia O'Keeffe's Vision." *The New Yorker,* March 4, 1974. https://www.newyorker.com/magazine/1974/03/04/the-rose-in-the-eye-looked-pretty-fine

General

Alameida, Roy Kākulu. "Nā Makani o Hawai'i." Hawaiian Studies Institute, May 1997. https://blogs.ksbe.edu/kekuiapoiwa/files/2013/09/Na-Makani-o-ka-Mokupuni.pdf

Areopagite, Pseudo-Dionysius. *The Divine Names and Mystical Theology.* Translated by John D. Jones. Milwaukee: Marquette University, 1980.

Augustine. *Confessions.* Translated by Henry Chadwick. Oxford: Oxford University Press, 1992.

Bachelard, Gaston. *Poetics of Space.* Boston: Beacon Press, 1969.

Blake, William. "To Thomas Butts" In *Blake Complete Writings,* edited by Geoffrey Keynes, 804. Oxford: Oxford University Press, 1979.

Burke, Edmund. *Philosophical Enquiry into the Origin of Our Ideas of the Sublime and Beautiful.* London: Dodsley, 1761.

Carroll, Lewis. *Alice's Adventures in Wonderland.* London: Macmillan, 2014.

Choi, Charles Q. "Faint Filaments of Universe-Spanning 'Cosmic Web' Finally Found." Space.com. October 3, 2019. https://www.space.com/universe-cosmic-web-filaments-found.html.

Conze, Edward, trans. *The Large Sutra on Perfect Wisdom.* Delhi: Motilal Banarsidass, 1979.

Dow, Arthur Wesley. *Composition.* Garden City, NJ: Doubleday, Page, 1913.

Emerson, Ralph Waldo. "Freedom." In *May-Day and Other Pieces,* 70. Boston: James R. Osgood, 1871.

Emerson, Ralph Waldo. "Nature." In *Selections from Ralph Waldo Emerson*, edited by Stephen Whicher, 21-56. Boston: Houghton Mifflin. 1960.

Fenollosa, Ernest. *The Chinese Written Character as a Medium for Poetry*. Edited by Ezra Pound. San Francisco: City Lights Books, 1936.

Feuchtwang, Stephen. *An Anthropological Analysis of Chinese Geomancy*. Vientiane, Laos: Vithagna, 1974.

Francis of Assisi. "The Canticle of Brother Sun." In *The Message of St. Francis*, edited by Sister Nan. New York: Penguin, 1999.

Frye, Northrup. *Fearful Symmetry: A Study of William Blake*. Princeton, NJ: Princeton University Press, 1947.

Galeano, Eduardo. "Origin of Sea Breezes," in *Mirrors: Stories of Almost Everyone*. New York: Nation Books, 2009.

Gregory, Andrew. *Early Greek Philosophies of Nature*. London: Bloomsbury Academic, 2022.

Guthrie, W. K. C. *A History of Greek Philosophy, Vol. 1: Earlier Presocratics and the Pythagoreans*. Cambridge: Cambridge University Press, 1962.

Gyatso, Geshe Kelsang. *Essence of Vajrayana*. London: Tharpa Publications, 1997.

Gyatso, Khedrup Norsang. *Ornament of Stainless Light: An Exposition of the Kalachakra Tantra*. Boston: Wisdom Publications, 2004.

Hamid, Mohsin. *Exit West*. New York: Riverhead Books, 2017.

Hannah-Jones, Nikole. "The Idea of America." *New York Times Magazine*, August 18, 2019.

Hefferman, James. 1995. *The Re-creation of Landscape: A Study of Wordsworth, Coleridge, Constable, and Turner.* Hanover, NH: University Press of New England, 1984.

Hepburn, Ronald. "The Aesthetics of Sky and Space." *Environmental Values* 19, no. 3 (August 2010): 273-288.

Hesiod. *Hesiod: Theogony, Works and Days.* Translated by Apostolos Athanassakis. Baltimore: Johns Hopkins University Press, 1983.

Hillman, James. "A Psyche the Size of the Earth." In *Ecopsychology*, edited by Theodore Roszak, Mary E. Gomes, and Allen D. Kanner, xvii-xix. San Francisco: Sierra Club Books, 1995.

Hillman, James. *The Thought of the Heart and the Soul of the World.* Dallas: Spring Publications, 1984.

Hopkins, Jeffrey. *Meditations on Emptiness.* London: Wisdom Publications, 1983.

Hui o Nā Wai ʻEhā "Kaulana ʻo Nā Wai ʻEhā" "Famous are the Four Great Waters of Waikapū, Wailuku, Waiehu, and Waiheʻe." https://www.huionawaieha.org/nawaiehainformation

Jewell, Edward Alden. "Brancusi Exhibition at Brummer Gallery Hard on Realists but Highly Pleasing to the Imaginative." *New York Times*, Nov. 18, 1933.

Jung, Carl. *Memories, Dreams, Reflections.* New York: Vintage Books, 1989.

Kloetzli, W. Randolph. *Buddhist Cosmology.* Delhi, India: Motilal Banarsidass, 1983.

Kodama, Kevin, and Steven Businger. "Weather and Forecasting Challenges in the Pacific Region of the National Weather Service." *Weather and Forecasting* 13 (September 1998): 523–546. http://www.soest.hawaii.edu/met/Faculty/businger/PDF/HawaiiFcsting.pdf.

Kukai. *Kukai: Major Works.* Translated by Yoshito Hakeda. New York: Columbia University Press, 1972.

ku'ualoha ho'omannawanui. *Voices of Fire: Reweaving the Literary Lei of Pele and Hi'iaka.* Minneapolis: University of Minnesota Press, 2014.

Kyselka, Will, and Ray Lanterman. *Maui: How It Came to Be.* Honolulu: University of Hawaii Press, 1980.

Macdonald, Gordon. *Volcanoes in the Sea.* Honolulu: University of Hawaii Press, 1983.

Malory, Thomas. *Le Morte d'Arthur.* Rendition by Keith Baines. New York: New American Library, 1962.

Marsh, Amy. *Le'ale'a O Na Poe Kahiko* - Joy of the People of Old Hawai'i. Electronic Journal of Human Sexuality, Volume 14, Feb. 14, 2011 http://www.ejhs.org/volume14/Joy.htm

McDougall, Brandy Nālani. *Finding Meaning: Kaona and Contemporary Hawaiian Literature.* Tucson: University of Arizona Press, 2016.

Michaels, Anne. "A Lesson from the Earth." In *The Weight of Oranges/ Miner's Pond.* Toronto: McClelland & Stewart, 1997.

Mookerjee, Ajit. *Yoga Art.* Boston: New York Graphic Society, 1975.

National Oceanic and Atmospheric Administration. "Why Does the Ocean Have Waves?" National Ocean Service website. Last updated January 20, 2023. https://oceanservice.noaa.gov/facts/wavesinocean.html

Neruda, Pablo, "Every Day You Play." In *Twenty Love Poems and a Song of Despair.* Translated by W. S. Merwin. New York: Penguin Books, 1976.

Newton, Isaac. *The Principia I.* Translated by Bernard Cohen and Anne Whitman. Berkeley: University of California Press, 1999.

"Newton's Laws of Motion." National Aeronautics and Space Administration. Last updated August 7, 2023. https://www.grc.nasa.gov/www/k-12/airplane/newton.html

Pabongka Rinpoche. *Liberation in the Palm of Your Hands.* Translated by Michael Richards. Boston: Wisdom Publications, 1991.

Paiva, Derek. "Hawai'i has 10 of the World's 14 Climate Zones: An Explorer's Guide to Each of Them." *Hawai'i Magazine,* Nov 10, 2015. https://www.hawaiimagazine.com/hawaii-has-10-of-the-worlds-14-climate-zones-an-explorers-guide-to-each-of-them/

Plato, "Theaetetus." In *The Dialogues of Plato. Vol. 2.* Translated by Benjamin Jowett. New York: Random House, 1937.

Plato, "Timaeus." In *The Dialogues of Plato, Vol. 2.* Translated by Benjamin Jowett. New York: Random House, 1937.

Raphael, H, "Aspect of the Heavens for January and February, 1939," *Publications of the Astronomical Society of the Pacific* 50, no. 298 (1938): 341. http://adsabs.harvard.edu/full/1938PASP...50..341R.

Rilke, Rainer Maria. *A Year with Rilke.* Translated and edited by Joanna Macy and Anita Barrows. New York: HarperOne, 2009.

Seiberling, Dorothy. "The Female View of Erotica." *New York Magazine 7,* February 1974.

Snyder, Gary. "Endless Streams and Mountains." In *Mountains and Rivers Without End.* Washington: Counterpoint, 1996.

Soseki, Muso. *Dialogues in a Dream.* Translated by Thomas Yūhō Kirchner. Somerville, MA: Wisdom Publications, 2015.

Stearns, H. T. *Geology of the Hawaiian Islands.* Honolulu: Territory of Hawaii and US Geological Survey, 1967.

Sterling, Elspeth. *Sites of Maui.* Honolulu, HI: Bishop Museum Press, 1998.

Suzuki, Shunryu. *Zen Mind, Beginner's Mind.* New York: Weatherhill, 1979.

Tilling, Robert, Christina Heliker, and Donald A. Swanson. "Plate Tectonics and the Hawaiian Hot Spot." Republished from *Eruptions of Hawaiian Volcanoes—Past, Present, and Future.* US Geological Survey, 2010. Geology.com. https://geology.com/usgs/hawaiian-hot-spot/.

US Army Corps of Engineers, "ʻĪao Stream Flood Control Project, Wailuku, Maui, Hawaiʻi," Honolulu: August 2021. https://www.poh.usace.army.mil/Portals/10/docs/Civil%20Works/ĪAO%20Stream%20FCP%20Repairs%20Aug%202021%20DRAFT%20EDR%20Amendment%20w%20Apps.pdf

Vasubandhu. *Abhidharma-kosa of Vasubandhu.* Translated by Subhadra Jha. Patna, India: K. P. Jayaswal Research Institute, 1983.

Vasubandu. *Abhidharmakośa-Bhasya of Vasubandu,* Vol. 1. Translated by Louis De La Vallee Poussin, Leo Pruden, and Gelong Lodrö Sangpo. Delhi, India: Motilal Banarsidass Publishers, 2012.

Vatsyanan, Kapila, ed. *Kalatattvakosa,* Vol. II. Delhi, India: Motilal Banarsidass, 1992.

Vernon, Mark. "The Say of the Land." *Aeon.* September 25, 2018. https://aeon.co/essays/words-have-soul-on-the-romantic-theory-of-language-origin.

Waley, Arthur. *The Way and Its Power: A Study of the Tao Te Ching and Its Place in Chinese Thought.* New York: Grove Press, 1958.

Wayman, Alex. *Yoga of the Guhyasamājatantra.* Delhi, India: Motilal Banarsidass, 1980.

Western Regional Climate Center. "El Nino / Southern Oscillation (ENSO) http://www.wrcc.dri.edu/enso/ensodef.html

Winters, Dennis. *Searching for the Heart of Sacred Space.* Toronto: Sumeru Press, 2014.

Wu, Katherine J. "Scientists Just Snapped the Best Image Yet of the Universe's Cosmic Web." Space.com. October 3, 2019. https://www.space.com/universe-cosmic-web-filaments-found.html

WATERFALL, NO I, ĪAO VALLEY, MAUI

WATERFALL NO. 1—ĪAO VALLEY—MAUI; WATERFALL—NO. 1—ĪAO VALLEY—MAUI; WATERFALL #1, ĪAO VALLEY, MAUI [DA]; WATERFALL, ĪAO VALLEY, MAUI NO. 1 [AN]

1939
Oil on canvas
19 x 16 (48.3 x 40.6)

Collection: Memphis Brooks Museum of Art, Memphis Tennessee;Gift of Art Today [purchase 1976] (76.7)

Provenance: (Doris Bry, New York, N.Y.)

Inscriptions: Stretcher: inaccessible
Verso: inaccessible
Backing:
1.   "Georgia O'Keeffe" (AS, black ink)
2.   "1939" (DB, blank ink)
3.   "14. Water Fall No. 1— Īao Valley—Maui" (AAP5)
4.   AAP11[twice]

Remarks: Source of first title: WA. WA indicates, "Painted 1939.

Exa. Amer. Place, March 1946." Titled *Waterfall #2, Ĩao Valley, Maui* in *New York Times* (February 1940). See cat. nos. 1914-16, 1923.

Conservation: "Sprayed with butyl methacrylate polymer, March, 1948. Be Keck" (Keck typed label).

Exhibitions: 1940 New York (An American Place—O'Keeffe), no 16, as *Water Fall —No.I—Ĩao Valley—Maui;* 1990 Honolulu, no. 17; 1998 St. Peterburg, no. 7

WATERFALL END OF ROAD, ĪAO VALLEY
WATERFALL—END OF ROAD— ĪAO VALLEY—HAWAII;
WATERFALL, END OF ROAD, ĪAO VALLEY [AN]

1939
Oil on canvas
19 x 16 (48.3 x 40.6)

Collection: Honolulu Academy of Arts Purchase, Allerton, Prisanlee, and Honolulu Advertiser,
Acquired with a gift from The Honolulu Advertiser, 1990 (8562.1)

Provenance: (Doris Bry, New York, N.Y.)
Private collection, Beverly Hills, California, 1973
Private collection, Hawaii, 1974
Estate of Doris Bry, New York, N.Y., 1983
Estate of Doris Bry, New York, N.Y., 1984
Private collection, Taos, New Mexico, 1987

Inscriptions: Stretcher: "End of Road— ĪAO Valley 1939 / (oil)" (AS, AAP2, black ink)

Remarks: Source of first title: WA. Not recorded DA. WA indicates:
"Reproduced and titled *Waterfalls of ĪAO* in *Vogue* (February 1941)."

Conservation: "Sprayed with butyl methacrylate polymer,
March, 1948, by Keck" (Keck typed label).

Exhibitions: 1940 New York (An American Place—O'Keeffe),
no. 15; 1986 San Francisco, no. 10; 1990 Honolulu, no. 20

WATERFALL, NO. 2, ĪAO VALLEY

WATERFALL—NO. II— ĪAO VALLEY;
WATERFALL, ĪAO VALLEY NO. II [AN]

1939
Oil on canvas
24 x 20 (60.1 x 50.8)

Collection: Private collection, Washington, D.C., 1972

Provenance: (The Downtown Gallery, New York, N.Y.)
Mrs. Iselin O'Donnell, New York, N.Y., 1947
Estate of Iselin O'Donnell, 1972
Sotheby Parke Bernet Inc., New York, N.Y., sale no. 3454,
lot no. 142, 13 December 1972

Inscriptions: Stretcher:
Verso:
Backing: "17. Water Fall—No. II—ĪAO Valley" (AAP5)

Remarks: Source of first title: WA. Not recorded DA. WA indicates:
"Exam. at Amer. Place, March, 1946." Reproduced and titled
Waterfall Number 2, ĪAO Valley, Maui, in *New York Times*
(February 1940).

Exhibitions: 1940 New York (An American Place—O'Keeffe),
no. 17, as *Water Fall—No. II—ĪAO Valley;* 1990 Honolulu, no. 18

WATERFALL, NO. III, ĪAO VALLEY

WATERFALL—NO. III— ĪAO VALLEY,
WATERFALL, ĪAO VALLEY NO. III [AN]

1939
Oil on canvas
24 x 20 (60.1 x 50.8)

Collection: Honolulu Academy of Arts,
Gift of Susan Crawford Tracy, 1996 (8562.1)

Provenance: (Doris Bry, New York, N.Y.)

Private collection, New York, N.Y., 1968
Private Collection, New York, N.Y., bequest, 1976
(De Graaf Forsythe Galleries, Ann Arbor, Michigan), 1979
Private collection, Ann Arbor, Michigan, 1979
Sotheby Parke Bernet Inc., New York, N.Y., sale no. 4290,
lot no. 234, 25 October 1979

Susan Crawford Tracy, Median, Texas, 1979

Inscriptions: Backing:
1.   "18. Water Fall—No. III—ĪAO Valley" (AAP5)
2.   "1939 / by Georgia O'Keeffe" (DB, black ink)

Remarks: Source of first title: WA. Not recorded DA.
WA indicates, "Exam. at Amer. Place, March 1946....
No signature" [notes inscription 1]. Titled *Waterfall* in
Park Avenue Social Review (1940).

Conservation: "Sprayed with butyl methacrylate polymer,
March, 1948, by Keck" (Keck typed label).

Exhibitions: 1940 New York (An American Place—O'Keeffe),
no. 18, as *Water Fall—No. III—ĪAO Valley*; 1990 Honolulu, no. 19

NOTES

Drawn from cited references and based upon documentation, the delineation of Georgia O'Keeffe's experiences and ideas are mine, as in note 125: "Selecting, deleting and emphasizing things imagined and felt. Nothing unreal nor untrue about that."

Having attempted to give proper credit for ideas and events not my own, to writers and writings from which and whom I've deviated to fit the book's momentum and my own thoughts, my apologies for inaccurate and/or insufficient citations. Where quotations and translations drawn from others are my iteration, notes state: "My iteration derived from ..."

1   Emerson, "Freedom," 70.

2   Jennings, *Georgia O'Keeffe's Hawai'i*, 20.

3   Paiva, "Climate."

4   Tompkins, "O'Keeffe's Vision."

5   See Tompkins, "O'Keeffe's Vision."

6   Seiberling, "Female View," 54.

7   Malory, *Le Morte d'Arthur*.

8   Hannah-Jones, "Idea of America," 26:

> "The eternity of the Atlantic Ocean had severed them so completely from what had once been their home that it was as if nothing had ever existed before, as if everything and everyone they cherished had simply vanished from the earth."

9   *Letters from O'Keeffe to Stieglitz.* Alfred Stieglitz / Georgia O'Keeffe Archive

10   Michaels, *Fugitive Pieces*, 71

11   *Letters from O'Keeffe to Stieglitz.* Alfred Stieglitz / Georgia

O'Keeffe Archive

12 Greenough, *My Faraway One*, 331, 353.

13 Vasubandu, *Abhidharmakośa-Bhasya*, 25, and Kloetzli, 1983, 24.

14 Western Regional Climate Center, viewed October 2018.

15 My iteration derived from Plato, "Theaetetus," 154.

16 My iteration derived from Hesiod, *Theogony*, 136–389.

17 Galeano, *Mirrors*, 112-113.

18 My iteration derived from Hesiod, *Theogony*, 179–231.

19 National Oceanic and Atmospheric Administration, "Why Does the Ocean Have Waves," and Suzuki, *Zen Mind, Beginners Mind*, 35.

20 Story told by Georgia O'Keeffe, *Georgia O'Keeffe*.

21 See Odall, *O'Keeffe and Texas*, 7–8, 16.

22 Derived from Haskell, *Abstraction*, 17,70, 193; Odall, *O'Keeffe and Texas*, 7,20; and Giboire, *Lovingly, Georgia*, 183.

23 Derived from various letters in Greenough, *My Faraway One*, 334, 381, 385.

24 See Greenough, *My Faraway One*, 690–691, 697, 703.

25 Marshall. *Nature and Abstraction*, 48

26 Georgia O'Keeffe, *Georgia O'Keeffe*, quoted with *Pedernal and Red Hills, 1936*

27 Dow, *Composition*, 44–45:
    "On a blank space, sketch out the main lines of the composition. This is called the Line-idea; on it hinges the excellence of the whole..."

28 Bachelard, *Poetics of Space*, 22, refers to "the dramatic tension between the aerial and terrestrial."

29 My iteration derived from Hesiod, *Theogony*, 136–389.

30 Winters, *Searching for the Heart of Sacred Space*, 203-204.

31 Raphael, "Aspect of the Heavens," 341.

32   Rilke, "Transforming Dragons" in *A Year with Rilke*, 191.

33   My iteration derived from Hesiod, *Theogony*, 289–301.

34   Snyder, *Mountains and Rivers Without End*, 5.

35   Hinton, *The Wilds of Poetry*, 2 writes, "Thoreau's questions about *who we are* and *where we are*..." and refers to this phrase and theme throughout the book.

36   Greenough, *My Faraway One*, 430.

37   See Dijkstra, *Eros of Place*, 5, 43, 57, 199–201 for the intimate relationship between Georgia O'Keeffe and landscape.

38   See Greenough, *My Faraway One*, 434, 477.

39   Bachelard, *Poetics of Space*, 192.

40   Hepburn, "The Aesthetics of Sky and Space," 275, refers to the difficulties of computing ideas of the cosmos.

41   Hefferman, *The Re-creation of Landscape*, 173.

42   Barson, *Georgia O'Keeffe*, 36–37. Also see *Music – Pink and Blue No. 1: 1918, Blue and Green Music 1919* and *Blue and Green Music 1921*

43   See Hillman, *Thought of the Heart*, 43–45.

44   Georgia O'Keeffe had painted *A Celebration 1924*. Following a flight to New Mexico, she was inspired to paint *Sky with Flat White Cloud 1962, Above the Clouds I, 1962-1963, Sky Above the Flat White Cloud II, 1960-1964, Sky Above the Clouds III / Above the Clouds III 1963*, and her largest, *Sky Above Clouds IV, 1965*.

45   See Greenough, *My Faraway One*, Odall, *O'Keeffe and Texas*, and Haskell, *Abstraction* for comments throughout.

46   Newton, *The Principia*, 408, 941.

47   See Charles Q Choi, "Faint Filaments," and Wu, "Cosmic Web Filaments."

48   Neruda, "Every Day You Play," 217

49   See Gregory, *Early Greek Philosophies*, 32, 69–70, 108–110, and Guthrie, *History of Greek Philosophy*, 87–88 for Anaximander's *apeiron*.

50   See Plato. "Timaeus 48–52," 28–32.

51   Refer to Augustine. *Confessions*, 121, 276–280, for his high regard for Plato, and his difficulty reconciling Plato's writings with his evolving ideas of Christianity.

52   Frye, *Fearful Symmetry*, 48.

53   Generally called Theravada, Mahayana and Vajrayana Buddhism.

54   The extensive Buddhist and Hindu references giving meaning to Space include: Conze, *Sutra on Perfect Wisdom*, 182, 184, 303, 307, 313, 352, 468, 487, 509; Gyatso, *Essence of Vajrayana*, 61, 178; Hopkins, *Meditations on Emptiness*, 66, 99, 217–219, 388–390; Wayman, *Guhyasamājatantra*, 20, 26–28, 48, 59, 110, 183, 209, 309; Vatsyanan, *Kalatattvakosa*, 93, 119; Vasubandu, *Abhidharmakośa-Bhasya*, 209.

55   My iteration derived from Wayman, *Guhyasamājatantra*, 313, in which I find "Space" more appropriate than Wayman's "sky.".

56   Rilke. "The Space Within Us" in *A Year with Rilke*, 41.

57   *Letters from O'Keeffe to Stieglitz*. Alfred Stieglitz / Georgia O'Keeffe Archive.

58   Saville, "Off in the Far Away," 103.

59   Sterling, *Sites of Maui*, 74.

60   Refer to Saville, "Off in the Far Away," 107 for combined March 15 and March 18 letters. "Down below" is my insertion.

61   Alameda, "Na Makani o ka Mokupuni."

62   Rilke, "Earth, Isn't This What You Want" in *A Year with Rilke*, 162.

63   Blake, *Blake Complete Writings*, 804. Blake wrote, "Are men seen from Afar."

64   This passage is humbly derived from McDougall, *Kaona*, 94.

65   Saville, "Off in the Far Away," 113

66   Refer to Kyselka and Lankerman, *Maui: How It Came to Be*, 36.

67   Derived from Tompkins, "Georgia O'Keeffe's Vision."

68   Refer to Hui o Nā Wai ʻEhā, viewed March 2024.

69   Groarke and Papanikolas, *Visions of Hawaiʻi*, 58; and US Army Corps of Engineers.

70   Oʻ Keeffe, *Georgia Oʻ Keeffe*, text accompanying "14 Music–Pink and Blue I, 1919."

71   Groarke and Papanikolas, *Visions of Hawaiʻi*, 63.

72   Refer to Jennings, *Georgia Oʻ Keeffe's Hawaiʻi*, 62–64; Saville, "Off in the Far Away," 110–114. Note chronological discrepancies among Patricia Jennings, Georgia Oʻ Keeffe's letters to Alfred Stieglitz and *Catalogue Raisonné* for the dates and order in which Georgia Oʻ Keeffe painted the four waterfalls and sketched the canyons. In personal conversations with Arnie Kotler, Koa Books publisher, he said that Patricia Jennings recalled Georgia Oʻ Keeffe's mixing up what took place and when. Lynes, *Catalogue Raisonné*, Vol. 1, 12:

"The bound sketchbooks in Volume 2 are arranged chronologically, based on the date of the first work found in each. Within a book, arrangement is based on page order, recto preceding recto, despite several books' containing works dating from more than a decade. Unbound sketches have been integrated into the chronology of the catalogue and, to the degree possible, grouped with works in other media to which they relate."

Here, I've credited Patricia's account for Georgia Oʻ Keeffe's painting *Waterfall No. 1* on Tuesday, March 21, 1939, the day following their arrival in Wailuku.

73   Oʻ Keeffe, *Georgia Oʻ Keeffe*.

74   See Tompkins, "Georgia Oʻ Keeffe's Vision."

75   Dow, *Composition*, 7–8:
"LINE refers to boundaries of shapes and the interrelations of lines and spaces. Line-beauty means harmony of combined lines or the peculiar quality imparted by special treatment. NOTAN, a Japanese word meaning "dark, light," refers to the

quantity of light reflected, or the massing of tones of different values. Notan-beauty means the harmony resulting from the combination of dark and light spaces—colored or not—in buildings, pictures, or in nature. Careful distinction should be made between NOTAN, an element of universal beauty, and LIGHT AND SHADOW, a single fact of external nature. COLOR refers to quality of light. These three structural elements are intimately related.

76   Greenough, *My Faraway One*, 174.

77   See Lynes, *Catalogue Raisonné*, Vol. 2, 1073, Image 1914, and Groarke, 2018, 30.

78   Sterling, *Sites of Maui.* 83–85.

79   Lynes, *Catalogue Raisonné*, Vol. 2, 1073, Images 1912, 1913.

80   See Lynes, *Catalogue Raisonné*, Vol. 2, 1073, for what I believe is Image 1915.

81   See Lynes, *Catalogue Raisonné*, Vol. 2, 1073, for Images 1916, 1917.

82   See Lynes, *Catalogue Raisonné*, Vol. 2, 1074, for Images 1919, 1921.

83   See Lynes, *Catalogue Raisonné*, Vol. 2, 1074, for Images 1920, 1922, 1923.

84   Greenough, *My Faraway One*, 381.

85   Groarke and Papanikolas, *Visions of Hawai'i*, 30.

86   Saville, "Off in the Far Away," 110

87   Elissa Gallander, conversation in the caldera of Genung Batur, Bali, April 1994.

88   See Tilling, Heliker, and Swanson, "Plate Tectonics."

89   Kyselka and Lankerman, *Maui: How It Came to Be*, 14–19.

90   Kyselka and Lankerman, *Maui: How It Came to Be*, 36.

91   I have no evidence that Georgia O'Keeffe experienced such an encounter or entered the caldera. None of her sketches appear to have been drawn within the caldera. This account is taken from my own experiences.

92   Kodama and Businger, *Weather and Forecasting*, 542.

93   Paragraph inspired by Hamid, 2017, 72.

94   See Bachelard, *Poetics of Space*, 213, for his discussion of *être-là*.

95   Carroll, *Alice in Wonderland,* 1–12.

96   My experience. The name of the temple was told to me by
        Nagata Masako, caretaker of the temple located on the
        mountain called Kompera-san, April 2001

97   O'Keeffe, *Georgia O'Keeffe.*

98   Bachelard, *Poetics of Space,* 223.

99   Francis of Assisi, "The Canticle of Brother Sun."

100   Suzuki, *Zen Mind, Beginners Mind,* 29.

101   See Kukai, *Kukai: Major Works.*

102   Emerson, "Nature," 32.

103   Jung, *Memories, Dreams, Reflections,* 335–336.

104   Gyatso, *Kalachakra Tantra,* 16.

105   O'Keeffe, *Georgia O'Keeffe*

106   Odall, *O'Keeffe and Texas,* 16, 22.

107   Refer to Lynes, *Georgia O'Keeffe in New Mexico,* 46, 51, 84, 87;
        Lynes, *Maria Chabot—Georgia O'Keeffe,* 4; and O'Keeffe, *Georgia
        O'Keeffe,* text with image 59 *Grey Hills II,* 1936.

108   Lynes, *Georgia O'Keeffe in New Mexico,* 51.

109   Saville, "Off in the Far Away," 110.

110   ku'ualoha ho'omannawanui, *Voices of Fire,* 5.

111   Winters, *Searching for the Heart of Sacred Space,* 63. For
        cosmological versions in Chinese history, see Waley, *The Way
        and Its Power* and Feuchtwang, *Chinese Geomancy.*

112   Derived from McDougall, *Kaona,* 94.

113   Stearns, *Geology of the Hawaiian Islands,* 5–8.

114   See Sterling, *Sites of Maui.* 81–82.

115   O'Keeffe, *Georgia O'Keeffe.*

116   Hillman, 1984, 43-45:
        "If beauty is essential to soul, then beauty appears whenever
        soul appears... Beauty is appearance itself. It is the way the
        Gods touch our senses."

117   O'Keeffe, *Georgia O'Keeffe.*

118   My iteration derived from Soseki, *Dialogues in a Dream,* 247-248

119   O'Keeffe, **Georgia O'Keeffe.**

120   Jewell, "Brancusi Exhibition," 13.

121   See Tompkins, "Georgia O'Keeffe's Vision."

122   See National Aeronautics and Space Administration, "Newton's Laws of Motion."

123   Pabongka Rinpoche, *Liberation in the Palm of Your Hand*, 554.

124   Hillman, "A Psyche the Size of the Earth," xvii–xix.

125   Barson, *Georgia O'Keeffe*, 246, note 54.

126   See Greenough, *My Faraway One*, 381.

127   See Areopagite, *The Divine Names*, 141.

128   Mookerjee, *Yoga Art*, Notes 24–34.

129   Burke, *Ideas of the Sublime and Beautiful*.

130   Hefferman, *The Re-creation of Landscape*, 188.

131   Jung, *Memories, Dreams, Reflections*, 335–336.

132   Greenough, *My Faraway One*, 334.

133   See Dijkstra, *Eros of Place*, 199–201.

134   Dijkstra, *Eros of Place*, 56–57.

135   Greenough, *My Faraway One*, 335:

"Critics were quick to recall Stieglitz's provocative nude portraits of O'Keeffe, exhibited only two years earlier, discussing her work in blatantly sexual terms. Stieglitz encouraged these interpretations, reprinting a Marsden Hartley ("Georgia O'Keeffe," 116-119) article in the exhibition brochure extolling O'Keeffe's paintings as 'shameless private documents [with an] unqualified nakedness of statement.'"

136   See Fenollosa, *Chinese Written Character*, regarding language based on the operations of nature and reflecting the temporal order in causation; and Vernon, "The Say of the Land."

137   See Fenollosa, *Chinese Written Character*. and Vernon, "The Say of the Land."

138   Neruda, "Every Day You Play," 53–55.

139   Waley, *The Way and Its Power*, 238. Nothing here is meant to

suggest dominance and recessiveness, superior and inferior, stronger and weaker. However, note the *Tao Te Ching*, Chapter LXXVIII:

"Nothing under heaven is softer or more yielding than water; but when it attacks things hard and resistant there is not one of them that can prevail. For they can find no way of altering it. That the yielding conquers the resistant and the softer conquers the hard is a fact known by all, yet utilized by none."

140   See Fenollosa, *Chinese Written Character*, 4–6.

141   O'Keeffe, *Georgia O'Keeffe*.

142   See Tompkins, "Georgia O'Keeffe's Vision."

143   Rilke, *A Year with Rilke*, 162.

144   Saville, "Off in the Far Away," 113.

145   Saville, "Off in the Far Away," 107.

146   Saville, "Off in the Far Away," 114.

147   Groarke and Papanikolas, *Visions of Hawai'i*, 36.

ABOUT THE AUTHOR

Dennis Alan Winters is an award-winning landscape architect with degrees in landscape architecture (Cornell) and architecture (University of Florida), and studies in urban design (Teknillinen Korkeakoulu, Helsinki). Through his studio, Tales of the Earth, he designs and builds gardens for meditation and writes about the sacred landscapes that inspire them, creating places of silence and the unbearable lightness of space. He is author of *Searching for the Heart of Sacred Space* (Sumeru, 2014), and contributing author to *Exploring Sexuality and Spirituality* (Brill, 2021), and *Architecture, Culture and Spirituality* (Ashgate, 2015).

He seeks stimulation in varied places and ways of living. In Helsinki to study architecture and urban design, he found the richness of farms, fields and forests. In Ithaca, New York, he discovered a spiritual home while documenting and analyzing the natural environment for local government. In Kathmandu to investigate the Himalayas, he made acquaintance with Tibetan Buddhism. And in Kyoto to study Japanese gardens, leading to research in Western Tibet, he was captivated by the sublimity of sacred landscapes. He's presented to UNESCO, Japan Society, Oxford University, Architecture, Culture and Spirituality Forum, and organized teachings for the Dalai Lama.

Making things with stone and wood helps him better understand qualities of the landscape, feeding his search for the 'truth of design'. As with his ingenious and original landscape designs, his writing serves as an inquiry into unconventional and mysterious things and thoughts. He lives on the escarpment shore of glacial Lake Iroquois in Toronto.

www.ingramcontent.com/pod-product-compliance
Lightning Source LLC
Chambersburg PA
CBHW031504120626
46545CB00005B/1752